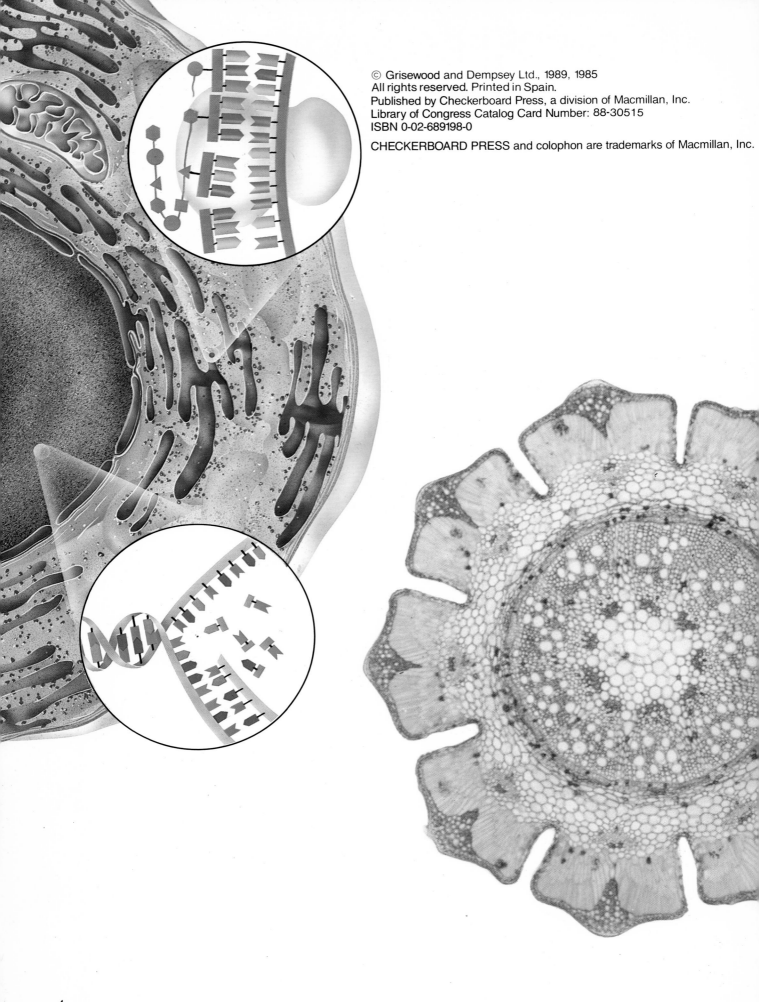

Published by Checkerboard Press, a division of Macmillan, Inc.
Library of Congress Catalog Card Number: 88-30515
ISBN 0-02-689198-0

CHECKERBOARD PRESS and colophon are trademarks of Macmillan, Inc.

CHECKERBOARD PRESS
Biology
Encyclopedia

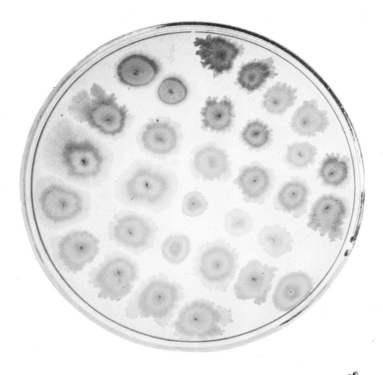

CHECKERBOARD PRESS
New York

Contents

AUTHORS
Edward Ashpole
Susan Jones
David Lambert

EDITOR
Barbara Taylor

COVER
Denise Gardner

6

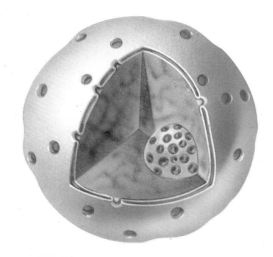

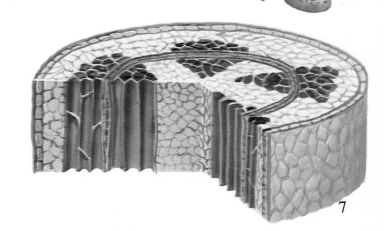

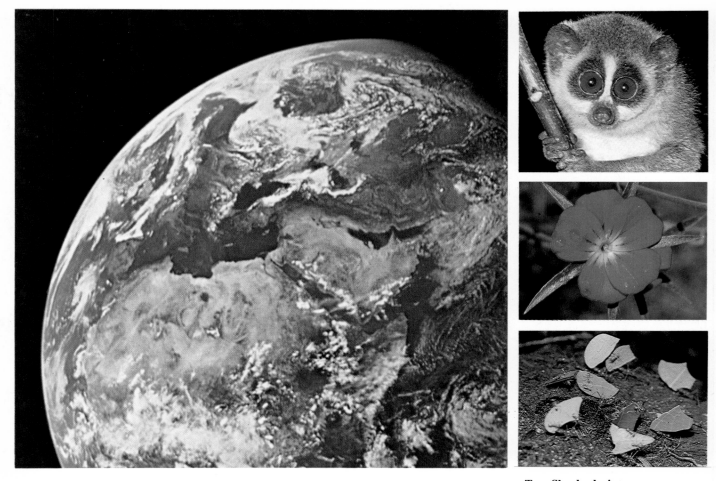

Top: Slender loris
Middle: Corn cockle
Bottom: Leaf-cutter ants

The Living Planet

From space our planet looks as if it is covered by a thin, bluish film. This is called the *biosphere* and it is what makes the earth different from all the other planets in our solar system. The biosphere includes all the places where life exists and it is much tougher than it looks. It was formed by life and it protects life. The soil in which plants grow, the oxygen we breathe and the protective layer of ozone (which shields all life on earth from deadly radiation from the sun) have all been produced by living things.

Within the biosphere, the chemical ingredients of life are used over and over again. They are taken out of the air or water by living things, built into living matter and returned to the atmosphere again when the bodies of plants and animals decay. They may also be locked up for some time in rocks or substances such as coal or oil. These substances may be released to the atmosphere again by natural chemical reactions or by people burning coal or oil.

Chemical elements such as carbon, oxygen, hydrogen and nitrogen have been recycled through the biosphere since the dawn of life more than 3.5 billion years ago. Some of the chemical elements in your body might have been part of a dinosaur or a fish millions of years ago. Without the bacteria and fungi that break down dead plants and animals, all the ingredients of life would remain locked up in dead creatures and the life cycles would come to a halt.

The Water Cycle
Water is vital to life. It is needed for all life processes and the hydrogen in water is one of the basic ingredients plants use to make their own food. The amount of water in the biosphere remains roughly the same because the water that escapes into the atmosphere from oceans, lakes and rivers falls back again as rain or snow. The whole cycle is powered by the sun, which provides the heat that makes water evaporate.

8

THE CARBON AND OXYGEN CYCLES

These two cycles are linked together. Plants take in carbon dioxide from the air to make new plant material and release oxygen in the process. This is called *photosynthesis* (see pages 66-67). Animals take in the carbon when they eat the plants. Both plants and animals take in oxygen to help them release energy from food. This is called *respiration* (see pages 42-43). Carbon dioxide is produced as a waste product and released to the atmosphere. Carbon and oxygen also return to the atmosphere when the bodies of plants and animals are broken down by bacteria and fungi and the chemical processes of decay. Some dead plants become compressed into a rock called coal. When people burn coal they use up oxygen and release carbon dioxide. Some carbon and oxygen from dead creatures and from the atmosphere becomes locked up in other rocks. This is released by chemical decay.

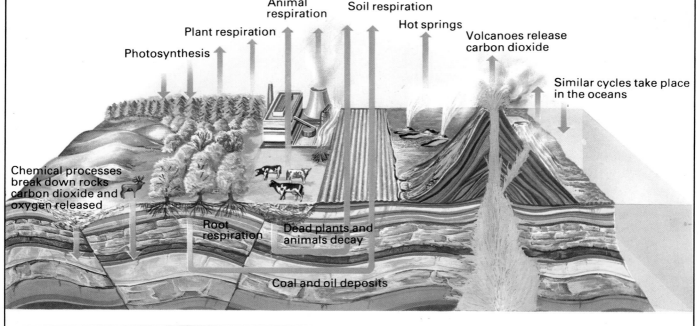

Animal respiration

Soil respiration

Plant respiration

Hot springs

Photosynthesis

Volcanoes release carbon dioxide

Similar cycles take place in the oceans

Chemical processes break down rocks carbon dioxide and oxygen released

Root respiration

Dead plants and animals decay

Coal and oil deposits

The Carbon Cycle

Carbon is the basis of all life on earth. It is recycled about once every 300 years. The main cycle is from carbon dioxide in the air to living matter and back to carbon dioxide again. This happens on land and in the sea. A large amount of carbon has become part of rocks and substances such as coal or oil. This carbon has taken much longer to return to the atmosphere than the carbon in living things. It is only returned when we burn these substances.

The Oxygen Cycle

Oxygen is recycled through the atmosphere about once every 2,000 years. Most of the oxygen in the atmosphere today comes from plants. They produce oxygen during the process they use to make their food from hydrogen and carbon dioxide (see pages 66-67). Advanced forms of life could not evolve on earth until simple plants had put enough oxygen into the atmosphere. A billion years ago only about one percent of the atmosphere was oxygen compared with about 20 percent today.

The Nitrogen Cycle

Although nitrogen is about 80 percent of the atmosphere, it cannot be used by most living things until it has been combined with hydrogen or oxygen. This job is carried out by bacteria. Animals take in chemicals that contain nitrogen when they eat the plants. The nitrogen is returned to the soil or the atmosphere when the bodies of plants and animals decay.

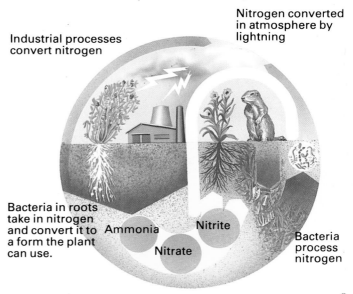

Nitrogen converted in atmosphere by lightning

Industrial processes convert nitrogen

Bacteria in roots take in nitrogen and convert it to a form the plant can use.

Ammonia

Nitrite

Nitrate

Bacteria process nitrogen

The Building Blocks of Life

What do you have in common with a fish, a tree, a mushroom or even a virus? At first sight, many forms of life on earth seem to have nothing in common except the fact that they are alive. There is such an enormous diversity of living things and they have adapted in a great variety of ways to their surroundings. Yet underneath all these differences lies a remarkable similarity.

All life on earth is made from the same chemical building blocks, which are called organic molecules. These are made mainly of carbon, nitrogen, hydrogen and oxygen. The organic molecule (*DNA*) is even used by all living things to code the instructions that control the way they live, grow and die. Could life be different on other planets? Perhaps it could. But there are good reasons for thinking that the basic chemistry of life may be the same.

In 1665 an English scientist called Robert Hooke discovered what living matter is made of. He looked at a piece of cork under a microscope and saw hundreds of little boxes. He called these boxes *cells*. All living things are made of one or more cells (apart from viruses – see pages 28-29). The human body is made up of about one hundred million million cells.

A cell is the smallest unit capable of life. Substances constantly stream into a cell. Chemical processes take place. Energy is released from food to fuel all of life's activities. The instructions for making more cells are copied. Yet although all these chemical processes are going on, a balance is maintained between input and output so that overall conditions stay the same. This is life. As the great French biologist Jacque Monod said 'Life is a process'.

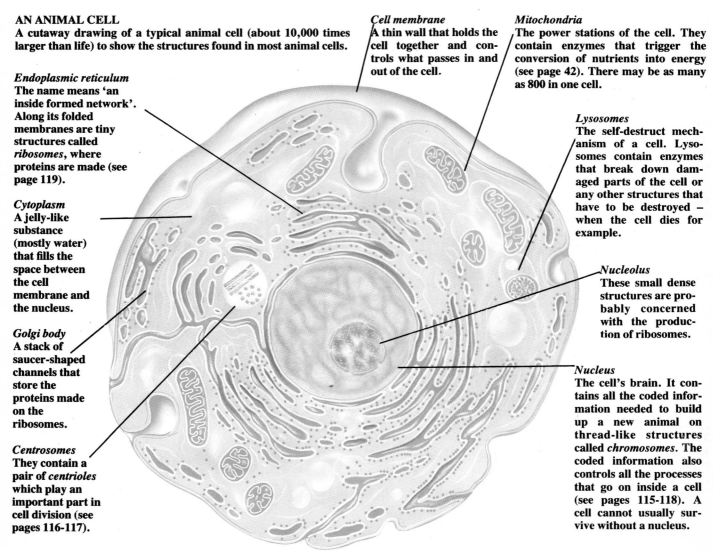

AN ANIMAL CELL
A cutaway drawing of a typical animal cell (about 10,000 times larger than life) to show the structures found in most animal cells.

Endoplasmic reticulum
The name means 'an inside formed network'. Along its folded membranes are tiny structures called *ribosomes*, where proteins are made (see page 119).

Cytoplasm
A jelly-like substance (mostly water) that fills the space between the cell membrane and the nucleus.

Golgi body
A stack of saucer-shaped channels that store the proteins made on the ribosomes.

Centrosomes
They contain a pair of *centrioles* which play an important part in cell division (see pages 116-117).

Cell membrane
A thin wall that holds the cell together and controls what passes in and out of the cell.

Mitochondria
The power stations of the cell. They contain enzymes that trigger the conversion of nutrients into energy (see page 42). There may be as many as 800 in one cell.

Lysosomes
The self-destruct mechanism of a cell. Lysosomes contain enzymes that break down damaged parts of the cell or any other structures that have to be destroyed – when the cell dies for example.

Nucleolus
These small dense structures are probably concerned with the production of ribosomes.

Nucleus
The cell's brain. It contains all the coded information needed to build up a new animal on thread-like structures called *chromosomes*. The coded information also controls all the processes that go on inside a cell (see pages 115-118). A cell cannot usually survive without a nucleus.

Animal and Plant Cells

Although each cell is usually specialized to carry out a particular job, all cells have certain features in common. You can see these features in the diagrams below. If you compare the animal cell with the plant cell you will see that they are made of more or less the same parts. But there are some differences.

Both plant and animal cells are enclosed in a protective membrane but plant cells also have a wall made of cellulose. A mature plant cell usually has a thin lining of cytoplasm and a large central cavity, called a *vacuole*, which is filled with cell sap. Animal cells consist almost entirely of cytoplasm and if they have any vacuoles, they are usually temporary and small. Many plant cells also have structures called *chloroplasts* (see page 66), which they use to trap the sun's energy to make their own food. Animal cells never have chloroplasts as they do not make their own food.

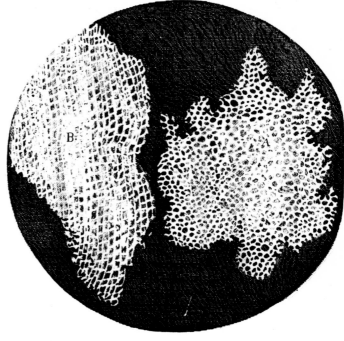

Above: This was the first drawing of cells ever made. The cells come from the corky layer near the surface of a piece of tree bark. They were observed by the English inventor and scientist, Robert Hooke, under a microscope which he made himself. Hooke published his drawing in *Micrographia* in 1665.

A PLANT CELL
A cutaway drawing of a typical plant cell. The structures which are the same as those in an animal cell are described on page 10.

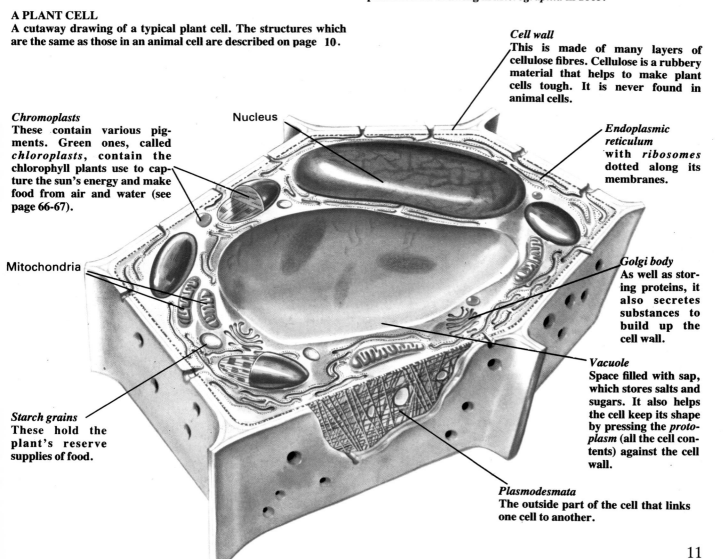

Chromoplasts
These contain various pigments. Green ones, called *chloroplasts*, contain the chlorophyll plants use to capture the sun's energy and make food from air and water (see page 66-67).

Nucleus

Mitochondria

Starch grains
These hold the plant's reserve supplies of food.

Cell wall
This is made of many layers of cellulose fibres. Cellulose is a rubbery material that helps to make plant cells tough. It is never found in animal cells.

Endoplasmic reticulum with *ribosomes* dotted along its membranes.

Golgi body
As well as storing proteins, it also secretes substances to build up the cell wall.

Vacuole
Space filled with sap, which stores salts and sugars. It also helps the cell keep its shape by pressing the *protoplasm* (all the cell contents) against the cell wall.

Plasmodesmata
The outside part of the cell that links one cell to another.

11

All Kinds of Cells

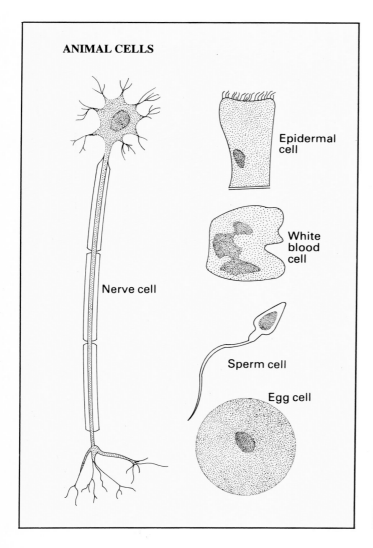

This microscopic one-celled organism is called *Paramecium*. It looks like a tiny speck to the naked eye. It is not the same as the single cells of many-celled animals because it is independent. It does not need other cells to survive. The surface of *Paramecium* is covered with tiny hair-like *cilia*, which beat together to move the animal through the water. The cilia also sweep tiny organisms, such as bacteria, into the gullet where they enter the cell to be digested. The star-shaped structures control water balance.

Cells come in a tremendous variety of shapes and sizes. For example, our red blood cells are only .0003 of an inch across while some of our nerve cells are 3 feet (a meter) long. Plants and animals that are made of many cells contain several different kinds. The human body contains many different kinds of cells, each with a particular job to do. The cells share the work rather like people share the work in a factory or office. Together they keep the factory or office working efficiently, and in the same way the cells work together to keep the body of a plant or animal working efficiently. This improves its chances of survival.

ANIMAL CELLS

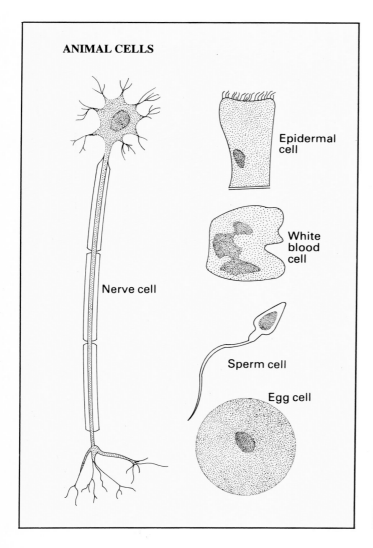

Nerve cell

Epidermal cell

White blood cell

Sperm cell

Egg cell

PLANT CELLS

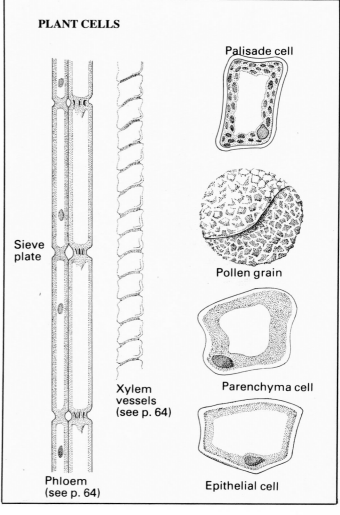

Palisade cell

Sieve plate

Xylem vessels (see p. 64)

Pollen grain

Parenchyma cell

Phloem (see p. 64)

Epithelial cell

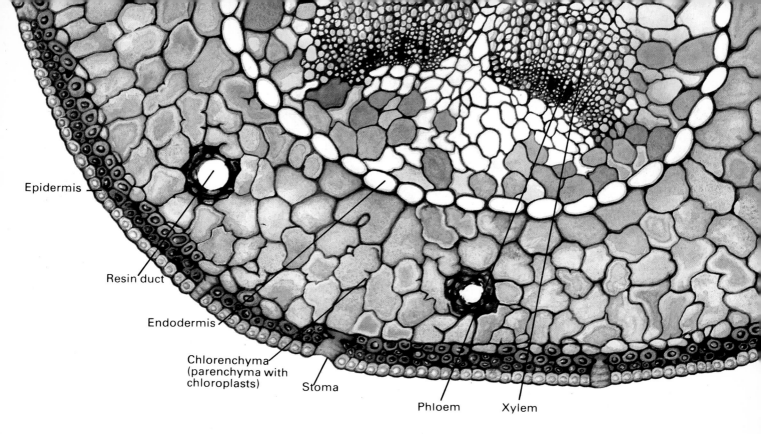

Epidermis

Resin duct

Endodermis

Chlorenchyma
(parenchyma with
chloroplasts)

Stoma

Phloem   Xylem

How Cells Work Together

In a plant or animal made of many cells, large numbers of cells of the same type are packed and held together to form *tissues*. For example, the human brain is made of nerve tissues composed of ten thousand million nerve cells connected to each other. In a complex plant or animal, different tissues are joined together to form *organs*, such as the heart or liver in humans, and leaves or flowers in plants. Some organs have just one job to do. The only job the heart does is to pump blood around the body. Other organs, such as the liver, have many tasks to carry out.

Organs and Systems

Some organs may work together to carry out particular tasks. These organs belong to a *system*. For example, in the human body, organs such as the intestine, the liver, pancreas and gall bladder make up the digestive system. Its task is to break down (digest) food so the nutrients can be absorbed into the body to provide us with energy.

Tissues, organs and systems appear very different in animals and plants. Yet the cells that they are made of contain the same basic structures – although no animal cell has chloroplasts for photosynthesis and no plant has nerve cells.

Above: A section through a pine needle as it would look under a microscope. You can see some of the different tissues which make up this plant organ. In the center of the leaf (at the top of the page) are the pipelines which carry food and water around the plant. The food pipes are called phloem and the water pipes are called xylem (see page 64). The two small circles near the edge of the leaf are resin ducts. On the very edge of the leaf are some openings called stomata (see page 65) which control the flow of air and water vapor in and out of the leaf.

Below: This diagram shows some of the main organs in the human body. An organ is a complex structure which has a particular task to carry out. It is made of a combination of tissues. Most tissues contain two or three types of cells mixed together.

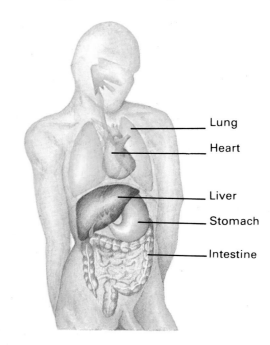

Lung

Heart

Liver

Stomach

Intestine

13

Animal Life

More than a million kinds of animal have been discovered on the earth so far. They range in size from microscopic one-celled animals to the gigantic blue whale, which grows up to 30 metres (98 feet) long. The blue whale is the largest animal ever to inhabit the earth.

Unlike green plants, animals cannot make their own food. They have to take it in ready-made by eating plants or other animals. Because of their need to find food, they have developed ways of moving around and responding to their surroundings.

Some microscopic living things can make their own food, like plants, but also take in ready-made food, like animals. They are not animals or plants and are sometimes grouped in a separate kingdom, called *protista*.

With or Without Backbones
Animals can be divided into those with backbones (*vertebrates*) and those without backbones (*invertebrates*). The vertebrates include the largest and brainiest animals, such as dolphins, elephants and human beings. The invertebrates are mostly very small creatures such as worms, snails and insects. But they outnumber the vertebrates by millions to one.

Animals Without Backbones
The simplest animals are one-celled organisms called *protozoa* – the name means first animals. There are thousands of different protozoa living almost everywhere, even inside or outside other animals. Protozoa are not the same as the cells that make up many-celled animals because they can survive on their own. They have no nerves or senses but they react to their surroundings as other animals do.

Sponges are groups of single cells that live as

Tube sponges from the Caribbean. Sponges draw water in and out through their many pores and filter out any food it contains.

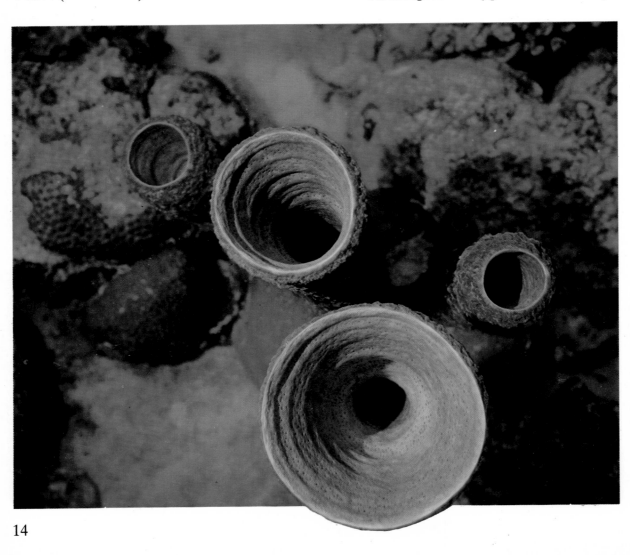

one animal. But if a sponge is broken up, the cells can come together again and new sponges will grow. Other many-celled animals could not survive being split up in this way.

The simplest many-celled animals are the sea anemones, jellyfish, corals and their relatives. They all live in water, mostly in the sea, and their ancestors can be traced back more than 500 million years. Biologists call them *coelenterates* – the name means hollow gut. They are rather like a sack into which they gather food with their tentacles.

A coelenterate is made of many different cells, which work together to keep the animal alive. It has body cells, reproductive cells, cells for stinging, cells that contract like muscles and a network of nerve cells. The coelenterates are the simplest animals to have nerve cells.

The simplest kind of worms are the *flatworms*. There are several thousand different kinds and they live in fresh and sea water and inside other animals. A flatworm has a gut, which is a simple food sack with only one opening.

Roundworms are an advance on flatworms. Most roundworms live freely in water or in soil,

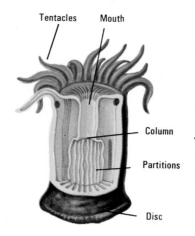

Tentacles Mouth

Column

Partitions

Disc

The inside of a sea anemone. The tentacles wave in the water to keep food particles flowing past. If a small animal touches the tentacles, stinging threads shoot out and paralyse it. (A jellyfish stings in this way.) The animal is then taken into the body cavity and digested in the partitions. The disc is used to grip on to rocks.

where they break down organic matter and release nutrients for plants to use. But some roundworms are serious parasites of plants and other animals. A roundworm has a mouth and a gut with an opening at the tail end (an anus) for getting rid of waste products.

The most advanced worms are the *annelids* or segmented worms, such as the earthworm. Their bodies are made up of round sections called segments and all their internal structures, such as blood vessels and nerve fibres, are repeated in each segment.

Right: Most adult coelenterates are attached to the seabed, like this living coral colony. Corals produce a hard, chalky skeleton for support and protection. This remains when the animal dies and new corals grow on top. After many generations, coral reefs or islands form.

Below: Earthworms push their way through soil, eating it as they go. The soil passes through the worm and any nutrients are taken out. Waste products are pushed out at the other end to form wormcasts. Earthworm tunnels help to mix up the soil layers and provide spaces for air to collect and water to drain away.

15

Above: A *crustacean* called a swimming crab. It uses its large pincers for picking up food. Crabs range in size from the tiny pea crabs (with shells only a quarter of an inch across) to the giant spider crab of Japan, which can measure 12 feet across its outstretched legs.

Above: An *insect* called a large tortoiseshell butterfly. Butterflies usually have feelers (antennae) with knobs on the end. Their relatives the moths usually have thread-like or feathery antennae. The wings of butterflies and moths are covered with colored or shiny scales. If you touch the wings the scales may rub off.

Below: A bird-eating spider, which is an *arachnid*. It can kill a small bird with its poisonous bite. Most spiders eat insects and only a few kinds (such as the black widow spider) are poisonous to humans. All spiders produce silk, which they spin from organs at the end of the abdomen called spinnerets. Most spiders use the silk as a safety line to help them move around. Some use the silk to make webs, which they use to trap insects.

Animals With Outside Skeletons

Animals with outside skeletons (*exoskeletons*) and many joints are the largest group of animals on earth. Biologists call them *arthropods* – *arthros* means "joint" and *podos* means "foot." The arthropods owe their great success to their small size and strong exoskeleton, which is made of *chitin* (animal plastic). Most biologists think all the arthropods evolved from worm-like creatures a few hundred million years ago. Some of the arthropods alive today, such as centipedes and millipedes, look similar to worms.

Most of the arthropods living in the sea, such as crabs and prawns, are *crustaceans*. A few crustaceans, such as the woodlouse, live on land, but they need a damp home. The most successful arthropods are the insects – more than three quarters of all animal species are insects. Many insects, such as bees, are useful to people but others, such as moths and termites, are pests. Some insects, such as mosquitoes, can carry disease.

The spiders and their relatives are called *arachnids* – *arachnes* means "spider." You can always tell an arachnid from an insect. Arachnids have 8 legs and a body in 2 parts. Insects have 6 legs and a body in 3 parts. Most insects can fly and have feelers called *antennae*. Arachnids never have antennae. Most spiders are harmless and are useful to us because they eat insect pests. But there are a few dangerous spiders in hot climates and some of the spiders' relatives are harmful. Mites and ticks suck blood and can cause disease.

From Snails to Squids

Mussels, oysters, whelks, snails, octopuses, and squid all belong to the second largest group of invertebrates, the *mollusks*. Some are only a tenth of an inch across while the giant squid, the largest of all invertebrates, can grow up to 66 feet (20 meters) long. Some mollusks (such as the snail) live in one shell, others (such as oysters and mussels) have two shells held together with a powerful "hinge."

The most advanced mollusks are the *cephalopods* – the name means "head and mouth." The cephalopods include the most intelligent of all invertebrates, the squid and octopuses. The cuttlefish is also a member of this group. You may know its skeleton, an internal shell shaped like a leaf, which is given to parakeets as a source of vitamins.

Animals Apart

The starfish, sea urchins and their relatives are unlike any other animals. Biologists call them *echinoderms* – the name means "spiky skin." There is evidence that they are related to the ancestors of the vertebrates, which lived in the seas some 500 million years ago.

Echinoderms have a completely different shape and structure from other animals. Their bodies are divided into five identical parts and they have a skeleton of plates inside their bodies. Echinoderms have no head or brain but they do have a system of nerves running through their bodies. They have no blood, so food and oxygen are carried to all parts of their bodies by water.

Above: The edible common whelk, which is a *mollusk*. It crawls around on its muscular foot and has a well developed head with eyes and tentacles.

Above: The common octopus can change color to match different backgrounds. Octopuses have eyes that are remarkably like ours, although they are quite unrelated to humans.

Below: A yellow-fringed sea slug (really a snail without a shell) feeding off sea anemones. It breathes through gill-like structures on its back.

Below: This *echinoderm* is a starfish called a sunstar.

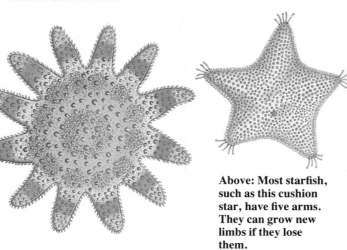

Above: Most starfish, such as this cushion star, have five arms. They can grow new limbs if they lose them.

Animals With Backbones

Fishes, the first animals with true backbones, evolved in the seas about 450 million years ago. There are three main groups of fishes today – the bony fishes (such as cod and herring), the cartilaginous fishes (such as sharks) and fishes with lungs. The lung fishes can breathe in air and underwater. This helps them to survive when the water they live in dries up from time to time.

The *amphibians* were the first vertebrates to walk on land. But they still need to go back to the water to breed and have to keep their skin moist. Amphibians, such as frogs, are cold blooded, which means their bodies are at the same temperature as their surroundings. In cold weather, they have to hibernate to survive.

The *reptiles* were the first true land vertebrates because they do not have to go back to the water to breed. They evolved from the amphibians about 300 million years ago and some of them, the dinosaurs, were amazingly successful. Today's reptiles are an insignificant bunch compared to those of dinosaur days. They include lizards, snakes, tortoises, turtles and the largest living reptile, the crocodile. Reptiles are also cold blooded and must hibernate in cold conditions. You may have a tortoise that has to hibernate each winter.

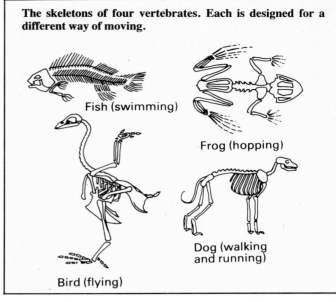

The skeletons of four vertebrates. Each is designed for a different way of moving.

Fish (swimming)

Frog (hopping)

Bird (flying)

Dog (walking and running)

Above: A grey shark, a fish with a skeleton made of cartilage and a skin covered in sharp spines.
Bottom right: The arrow poison frog secretes a powerful poison from its skin.
Bottom left: A lizard called a green iguana. Like all reptiles, it has a scaly skin so it does not lose water easily.

The fish eagle lives all over Africa south of the Sahara desert. It catches fish in its sharp talons as it flies slowly over the surface of the water.

Birds evolved from reptiles about 150 million years ago. You can still see the reptile in birds in their scaly legs. By inventing feathers birds have been able to conquer the air. No other animal can fly half way round the world and back. But to fly like a bird uses a lot of energy. Birds have large hearts to keep their flying muscles well supplied with food and oxygen. Their body temperature is higher than ours because they burn up food faster to release energy more quickly. We would die from fever if our temperature reached that of birds.

Like the birds, *mammals* also evolved from the reptiles. They did not become the major group of animals on earth until the dinosaurs died out about 65 million years ago.

There are three main kinds of mammal. *Placental* mammals (such as humans) where the young stay inside their mother's womb until they are fully formed, *marsupials* (such as kangaroos) which bear their young at an early stage of development, and *monotremes* which are unusual mammals that lay eggs. The only living monotremes are the platypus and spiny anteater of Australasia. All mammals are warm blooded (which means they can control their body temperature) and they have fur or hair. Mammals also have better brains and are more intelligent than any other animals.

Above: A common dormouse (a placental mammal) at its summer nest in a bramble bush.
Bottom left: The platypus is an unusual Australian mammal. It uses its sensitive bill to hunt for small animals in rivers.
Bottom right: A newly-born kangaroo (only 4 centimetres long) feeding from a teat in its mother's pouch.

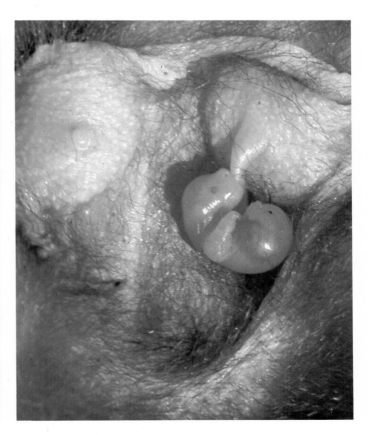

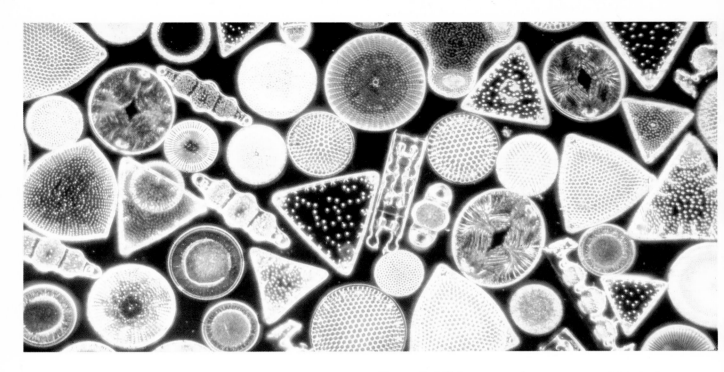

Plant Life

Green plants connect life on earth to its energy source, the sun. They capture energy from sunlight using *chlorophyll*, which is the substance that gives most plants their green color. They use the energy to make food in a complex chemical process called *photosynthesis* – the word means "making things with light."

Animals cannot make their own food so they have to eat plants, or eat animals that have eaten plants. (We only eat steak because cows eat grass.) The process of photosynthesis releases oxygen into the atmosphere. So plants not only feed us, but they enable us to breathe as well.

Algae

The simplest plants are the *algae*. They have no roots, stems or leaves and most of them are made of just one cell. Plants similar to today's single-celled algae evolved in water more than two and a half billion years ago.

Algae in the oceans carry out most of the photosynthesis on earth. This is not really surprising because oceans cover nearly 70 percent of the earth's surface. The algae float in the surface waters and form part of what biologists call *plankton*. Plankton is the basis of all nutrition in the sea. It even feeds some of the great whales.

Algae called diatoms are an important part of the plankton in the oceans. Their silica shells are often shaped into the most amazing patterns.

Algae exist in water or damp places almost everywhere. A single-celled alga called *Chlamydomonas* sometimes turns the surface of ponds and streams green. Seaweeds, a common feature of seashores all over the world, are also algae. They are made of many cells. Some of them can grow up to 50 feet (15 meters) long. Did you realize that the green powdery film you often see on trees and old wooden fences is caused by an alga called *Pleurococcus*? This is one of the few algae that can survive away from water.

Many seaweeds contain red or brown pigments to help them capture the particular wavelengths of light energy from the sun that reach them underwater.

Coral weed

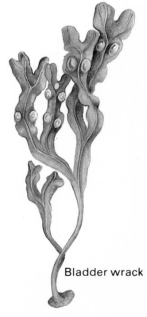

Bladder wrack

20

Moving on to Land

Plants began to colonize the land about 500 million years ago. But they had problems to overcome. Water plants are supported by the water all around them. The gases they need for breathing and photosynthesis are dissolved in the water in a form easily taken in. Their seeds are carried away by the flow of the water.

But land plants have to hold themselves upright against the earth's gravity. They have to take in water and gases from the air and soil and transport food and water around inside their bodies. Their seeds have to be carried away by the wind or animals. And they must avoid being dried out by the sun and wind.

The simplest land plants are the *liverworts*, which have this name because they are supposed to be shaped like a liver. They are very common in damp places.

Right: A few ferns, such as this one from Tahiti, grow to the size of trees. Their "trunks" are the remains of old dead fronds (leaves).

Above: The European hard fern carries its spores on special fronds that stand upright in the center of the plant.

Above: Liverworts have no leaves, stems or roots. They consist of a plant body fixed to the ground by thread-like cells, called *rhizoids*.
Below: The leaves of sphagnum mosses have large empty spaces, which hold large amounts of water.

Mosses have stems and leaves but no actual roots. Most mosses are only about an inch high. Like liverworts, they are fixed to the ground by hair-like structures called *rhizoids*. Their rhizoids can break up rock or stone surfaces and help soil to form. Other plants may then be able to grow in this soil.

Ferns have leaves called *fronds*, which usually grow from underground stems called *rhizomes*. Roots anchor the plant in the soil. Ferns were the dominant life form on earth between 400 and 300 million years ago, when the first animals were appearing on the land. Much of the coal mined today is the preserved remains of the great fern forests of that time. Ferns and their relatives were the first plants to develop a system of tubes for transporting food and water around inside their bodies. These tubes are like our arteries and veins.

21

Mature female cones of the sitka spruce, which is widely planted for its timber.

Left: A giant redwood tree in North America. One of these trees is the largest living thing on earth. These trees can grow more than 90 metres high and some have lived for four thousand years. The bark of the trees is thick and spongy. This helps them to withstand the heat of forest fires.

Plants With Cones

A remarkable group of plants called the *gymnosperms* evolved after the ferns. These were the first plants to produce real seeds – the word gymnosperm means 'naked seed'. Most of the gymnosperms are conifers, which were the main plant group on earth 250 million years ago.

Conifers are still very common today and include trees such as the pines and redwoods. They have needle-like leaves (which they keep all year round) and their seeds grow in protective cones. The scales of the cones open in spring so that reproductive cells (pollen) from the male cones can fertilize the reproductive cells in the female cones. The scales close again while the seeds develop but open again to release the ripe seeds. These are carried away by the wind or by animals that eat them.

Flowering Plants

The flowering plants evolved some 150 million years ago and are the most successful group of plants on the earth today. They have outstripped

Black mulberry   Bittersweet   Laburnum

Horse chestnut   Pomegranate

Above left: Birds and other animals eat fruits but the seeds inside pass through their bodies unharmed and may grow into new plants.

Above right: This beautiful bee orchid *Orchis apifera* attracts male bees by looking and smelling like a female bee. The bees may pick up some of the orchid's pollen and carry it to another flower (see page 73).

all other plants in their spectacular variety and, above all, have perfected the production of seeds. Biologists call them *angiosperms*, which means 'container seeds'.

The special inventions of flowering plants, their flowers, fruits and nuts, are ways of improving the process of reproduction. Many flowers have bright colours, scents or shapes to attract the right animals, especially insects, to carry their pollen from flower to flower. Putting the seeds inside fruits and nuts works in a similar way to persuade birds and mammals to visit them and carry the seeds away. The evolution of animals and flowering plants has been closely linked, with each helping the other to survive. The search for fruit in the trees probably influenced the evolution of our ancestors, the monkeys and apes.

Some flowering plants rely on the wind to carry their pollen and seeds. Their flowers, such as tree catkins or grass flowers, are not colourful or scented and their seeds are light and may have special structures to help them float on the wind.

Flowering plants have evolved a variety of roots, stems and leaves, and some have taken on special jobs. Large taproots (such as carrots), swollen stems (such as potatoes) and fleshy leaves (such as onions) all store food for the plants as well as carrying out their other tasks. Some of the leaves of roses have developed into thorns to protect the plant. Many leaves of flowering plants are good to eat. None of the grazing animals could have evolved without the grasses they feed on.

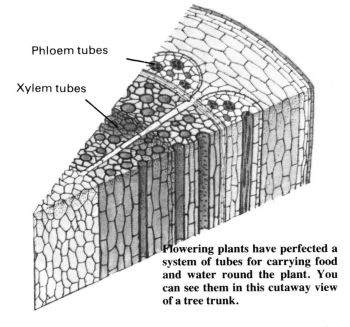

Phloem tubes

Xylem tubes

Flowering plants have perfected a system of tubes for carrying food and water round the plant. You can see them in this cutaway view of a tree trunk.

23

Fungi

The *fungi* are an ancient and separate kind of life. They are not plants because they have no chlorophyll and cannot make their own food. They are also built differently from plants. Fungi have no stems, leaves or roots and no cell walls of cellulose. The nearest relatives of the fungi are the bacteria. The fungi probably evolved from this simple lifeform a few hundred million years ago.

Fungi get their food directly from living or dead plants and animals. They cause many serious diseases in plants (such as mildews on food crops) and a few diseases in animals. The most common disease we get from fungi is athlete's foot, which causes the skin between our toes to crack.

Millions of people owe their lives to the most common kind of fungus, the molds. In 1928 Alexander Fleming discovered by chance that a mold produced a substance that killed certain bacteria. The name of the mold was *Penicillium notatum* and the substance it produced was called penicillin. It was the first antibiotic prepared for medical use. Since that time, biologists have found that other fungi produce their own kind of antibiotics and doctors now have a large range of antibiotics to treat different bacterial diseases.

The poisonous fly agaric toadstool usually grows on birch tree roots. It has a special give-and-take relationship with the tree. (This is a form of symbiosis – see page 88.) The fly agaric obtains sugars from the tree and in return provides the tree with nutrients it cannot easily get from the soil. Both partners benefit from living together in this way.

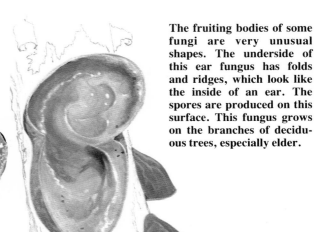

The fruiting bodies of some fungi are very unusual shapes. The underside of this ear fungus has folds and ridges, which look like the inside of an ear. The spores are produced on this surface. This fungus grows on the branches of deciduous trees, especially elder.

Below: Fungus spores are everywhere in the air. This is why moist food becomes moldy so quickly.

There are about 90,000 species of fungi ranging from microscopic single cells, such as yeasts, to large mushrooms and toadstools. Yeasts are very important to people because they break down sugars, making alcohol and carbon dioxide gas in the process. They are used to make wine and beer and the carbon dioxide they produce makes bread rise.

The above-ground parts of mushrooms and toadstools are the structures of reproduction. They carry out the same job as the microscopic pinheads of the molds – they hold billions of *spores*, which are blown away by the wind. The body of the mushroom or toadstool is a mass of fine threads under the ground.

Lichens

Some fungi have overcome the problem of not being able to make their own food in an unusual way. They have evolved a close relationship with algae, which live within the fungus.

The fungus provides the algae with protection and water. The algae use sunlight to make food for themselves and the fungus. This group of fungi are called lichens. The shape of the lichen depends on the shape of the fungus. Some lichens look like flat patches of color while others are leafy and stubbly. A close relationship between two different life-forms in which both partners benefit is called *symbiosis* (it means "living together") – see pages 88-89.

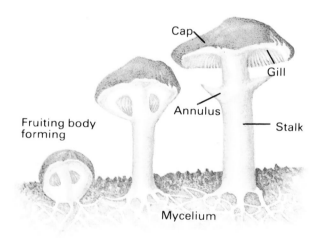

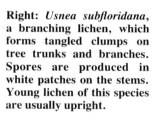

Above: The body of a fungus is called a *mycelium*. It is made up of a mass of fine threads called *hyphae*. The hyphae produce enzymes, which break down the food into a form the fungus can absorb. Sometimes the hyphae weave together to form mushrooms and toadstools above ground. These structures carry the spores of the fungus and often appear in autumn.

Below: A water droplet splashing on to this earthstar, *Geastrum triplex*, has released a cloud of billions of spores.

Xanthoria parietina, a leafy lichen, which is common on rocks and old walls, especially near the sea. Spores are formed in the darker patches in the center of the lichen.

Right: *Usnea subfloridana*, a branching lichen, which forms tangled clumps on tree trunks and branches. Spores are produced in white patches on the stems. Young lichen of this species are usually upright.

Below: Map lichens growing on a rock. Individual plants have black edges, which join together like the lines drawn on maps.

Bacteria

Bacteria are everywhere – in the air we breathe, on and inside our bodies, in soil, fresh water and the sea. They can even live on iron, sulphur and other non-living materials. It is estimated that all the bacteria in the world would weigh 20 times more than the weight of all other living things put together.

Bacteria are single cells and the smallest form of life on earth. A microscope with high magnification is needed to study individual bacteria. A drop of water may contain thousands of bacteria, while there may be a million in a drop of sour milk.

Bacteria have a distinct structure and are unlike other single cells. They have a rigid outer shell (cell wall) made of *chitin*, which is covered by slime and mucus. (Chitin is the very strong material used by insects and other arthropods for their exoskeletons.) Inside the chitin shell is an inner cell membrane enclosing the usual structures found in cells. This includes the special chemicals that carry the genetic information of the bacteria. But this genetic material is not enclosed in a nucleus as it is in plant and animal cells.

Round bacteria linked in chains. **Rod-shaped bacteria** **Bacteria with fine threads to help them move.**

AFTER 6 HOURS **AFTER 9 HOURS**

Above: Bacteria can reproduce very rapidly. In good conditions, they can divide every 30 minutes. At this rate, a single bacterium would leave 280,000,000,000,000 descendants at the end of 24 hours.
Below left: A microscopic view of chains of the bacterium *Ruminococcus flavefaciens* in the grass cells in the stomach of a cow. The bacteria break down the cellulose of the grass cells into sugar. Some of the sugar is used by the bacteria but the rest is absorbed by the cow.
Below right: Rod-shaped bacteria *Lactobacillus bulgaricus* as they appear under a high power microscope.

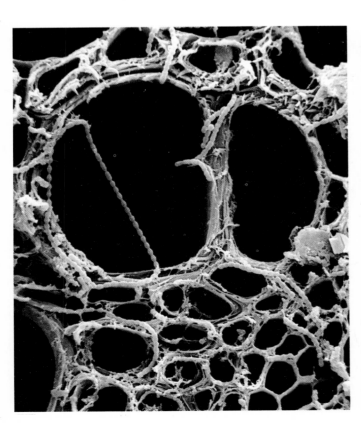

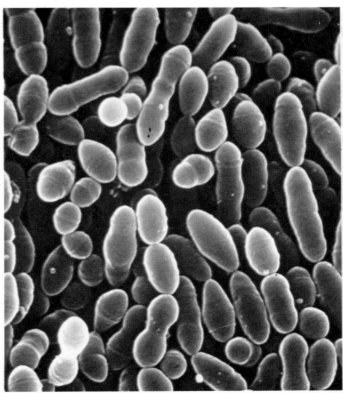

Above: Louis Pasteur at his clinic. He was one of the first scientists to prove that some diseases were caused by particular microbes. This idea is called the *germ theory* of disease and in the 1860s and 1870s it seemed a revolutionary idea. Before this theory was accepted, all sorts of strange ideas (such as supernatural influences and the character of the sick person) had been used to explain diseases.

Right: During the 20th century, people have controlled many harmful bacteria with drugs and antibiotics.

Bacteria and Disease

The first person to see bacteria was a Dutchman, Anton van Leeuwenhoek. In 1683 he saw what he described as 'animacules' or 'little eels' in a drop of rainwater under a simple microscope. However, almost a hundred years passed before Leeuwenhoek's work led to some practical ideas. In 1762 an Austrian doctor, Anton von Plenciz, suggested that bacteria cause diseases and that different diseases are caused by different bacteria. But Plenciz was not shown to be correct until the middle of the last century.

Robert Koch of Germany (1843-1910) was able to link certain bacteria to the diseases they cause. He found the *bacillus* (a rod shaped bacterium) that causes tuberculosis, which was a major killer before the age of antibiotics.

Louis Pasteur of France (1822-1895) showed that decay and infection were caused by microscopic living things, including bacteria. Pasteur's research led to vaccines against bacteria. He showed that vaccines of dead bacteria could be used to stimulate the body's natural defences against bacteria. He was also asked to solve the problem of wine being soured by bacteria. He found that bacteria could be killed by heating the wine to a temperature below the boiling point. This work led to the widespread use of the process known as *pasteurization*, which protects people from harmful bacteria in milk and other foods.

Fortunately most bacteria are harmless. Only a few dangerous ones cause diseases. And many bacteria live with us and are essential for our health. We could not live without the vast quantities of bacteria in our gut, which help us to digest our food. Bacteria also feed on dead plants and animals and play a vital role in breaking down their bodies and making the chemicals in them available for new life.

27

Viruses

At the end of the last century, biologists discovered that fluids from sick animals could be used to cause diseases in healthy animals, although they contained no bacteria or any other cells. The mysterious agents of disease turned out to be *viruses*. They could not be seen until the development of powerful electron microscopes.

Viruses are built differently from all living things. They are the only life-forms that are not made of one or more cells. They consist mainly of *nucleic acids* (genetic materials) with a coating of large protein molecules. The nucleic acid molecules contain the building plans for a new virus. In this respect, viruses are exactly like all living things. Every organism has its own plans coded in nucleic acid molecules that are copied and handed on from generation to generation.

But, unlike living things, viruses cannot make copies of their plans and produce new viruses on their own. They have to invade a living cell and use this cell's "machinery" in order to reproduce themselves.

Yet viruses are particular. They do not invade any cell. Each kind of virus only invades certain types of cells in particular animals or plants. For example, cold viruses invade the cells of the nose or throat in human beings but will not affect those cells in your cat or dog. Even bacteria have their own viruses.

Above: A potato plant with leaf roll virus. This makes the leaves so dry that they rattle if the plant is shaken.

Above: A virus causes the white streaks in these pink tulips. It reduces the amount of pigments in the petals.

Left: This is what a virus called a bacteriophage looks like under the electron microscope. Bacteriophages attack bacteria. They attach themselves to the bacteria with their tail section. Then they inject their nucleic acids (which are stored in the head section) into the bacteria.

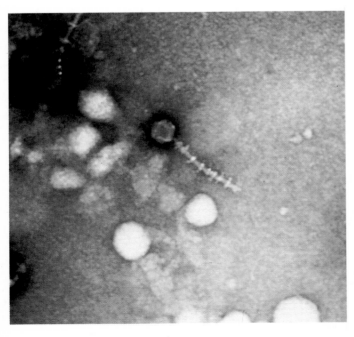

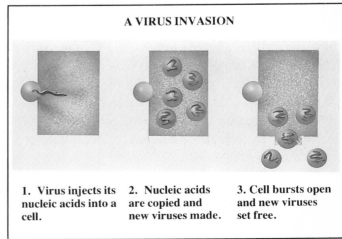

A VIRUS INVASION

1. Virus injects its nucleic acids into a cell.

2. Nucleic acids are copied and new viruses made.

3. Cell bursts open and new viruses set free.

Viruses and Disease

Viruses cause many diseases in plants and animals. They include influenza, mumps, measles, polio, rabies, foot-and-mouth disease in cattle and myxomatosis in rabbits. The big problem with viruses is that they cannot be knocked out by drugs as bacteria can. But if a plant or animal suffers from a viral infection, its body develops a natural defense against that disease and this protects it against further attacks.

An injection of dead or subdued viruses (a *vaccination*) stimulates these natural defense systems in the same way. So vaccinations can protect people against serious attacks by viruses. This is the only way to fight these diseases unless medical scientists learn how to block the way viruses work inside cells and prevent them taking over cells to produce more viruses. But this is difficult because it has to be done without affecting the workings of the cell under attack.

Not all viruses cause disease and even those that do sometimes lie dormant and have no effect at all. Almost all tissues of animals and plants contain viruses and many seem to cause no trouble. There is still much scientists do not understand about viruses and they are a major subject for modern research.

Above: The most common viral disease, the common cold, is caused by too many varieties of the virus for medical scientists to prepare a vaccine. When people catch colds, it usually takes about three days for the body's natural defenses to overcome the invading viruses.

Below left: Polio viruses seen through a very strong microscope. Polio attacks the brain and spinal cord.
Below right: An Iranian boy being vaccinated against tuberculosis. Edward Jenner, an English doctor, began the use of vaccine injections to protect people against viral diseases. Mass vaccination campaigns have stopped many people from catching some of the worst infectious diseases.

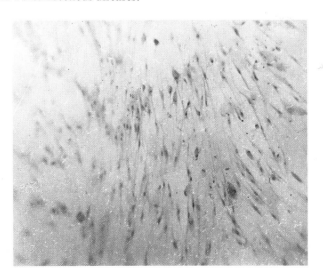

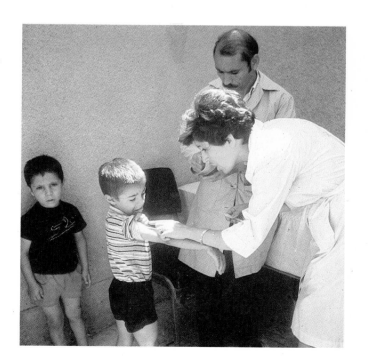

The Body Framework

Animals have to support and protect their soft tissues and organs. Some soft-bodied animals, such as jellyfish, are supported by the water they float in. Others, such as worms, keep their shape because of the pressure of the fluids inside them. But most animals support their bodies with a framework called a *skeleton*.

All vertebrates have skeletons inside their bodies. This 'inside skeleton' can be made of bone or cartilage. Some fishes, such as sharks, have skeletons of cartilage throughout their lives. The skeletons of all vertebrate embryos (including those of humans) are made mostly of cartilage to begin with. This is gradually replaced by bone during growth and development but the process is not completed in humans until the age of about 25. The skeleton in some parts of our bodies (such as the end of our nose and our earlobes) remains as cartilage throughout our life.

What are Bones Made of?

Bones are made of two different types of material – hard minerals, containing calcium and phosphorus, and flexible living protein, called *collagen*. This makes bones strong but at the same time bendy enough not to snap easily. Cracks in the hard bone minerals cannot travel easily through the flexible collagen. As people get older, the rubbery collagen is replaced by hard minerals so the bones become more brittle and break easily.

Blood vessels and nerves are contained in tiny canals that run through bones. The blood carries food, oxygen and waste products to and from living cells in the bone. At the centre of many bones (such as your leg bones) is a hollow with soft tissue, called *marrow*, inside. Red marrow, which is found only in mammals, produces blood cells – it produces red blood cells at the rate of about 2.5 million cells every second.

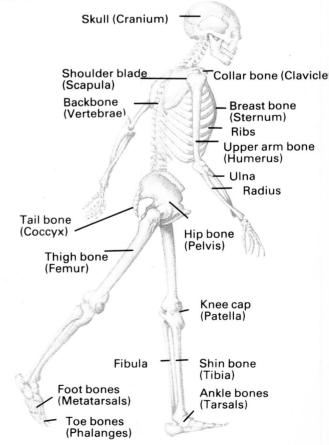

Left: A giant bone from a dinosaur called *Camarasaurus* being uncovered at the Dinosaur National Monument, Utah, USA.
Below: Your skeleton is a framework which supports your body and protects the delicate organs inside. You have over 200 bones in your skeleton. Your largest bone is the thigh bone and your smallest bones are in the middle ear.

Skull (Cranium)
Shoulder blade (Scapula)
Collar bone (Clavicle)
Backbone (Vertebrae)
Breast bone (Sternum)
Ribs
Upper arm bone (Humerus)
Ulna
Radius
Tail bone (Coccyx)
Hip bone (Pelvis)
Thigh bone (Femur)
Knee cap (Patella)
Fibula
Shin bone (Tibia)
Foot bones (Metatarsals)
Ankle bones (Tarsals)
Toe bones (Phalanges)

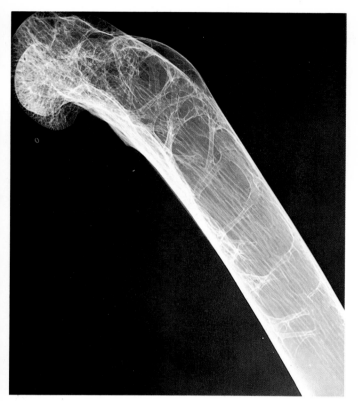

Above: X-ray of a bone from a pelican, showing the many air passages. Hollow bones help to cut down a bird's weight so it needs less energy to fly.

Top right: X-ray of human shoulder joint.
Bottom right: X-ray of human pelvis.
Both these X-rays reveal ball and socket joints, which allow movement in many directions.

Above: The empty exoskeleton of a dragonfly nymph.

Outside Skeletons

The skeletons that some animals (such as insects) wear outside their bodies are made mainly of *chitin*. This material is tough, hard and waterproof and provides good protection. Muscles attached inside the skeleton allow the animals to move. But there is one major disadvantage to an outside skeleton, which is that it cannot stretch as the animal grows. It has to be shed from time to time and replaced with a larger skeleton. While this is happening the animal is not protected from attack.

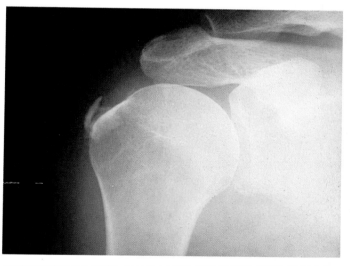

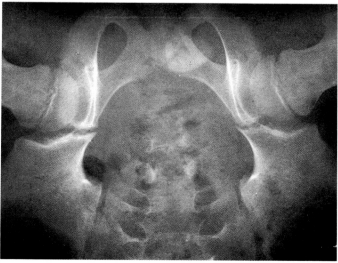

LOOKING AT JOINTS

The place where two bones meet is called a *joint*. Some joints, such as those between the bones in your skull, have grown together so tightly that they are fixed. But most joints are movable. In a movable joint, muscles and tough straps called *ligaments* hold the bones together. The ends of the bones are coated with a smooth protein called *cartilage*. The joint is surrounded by a thin, slippery membrane. This produces a special fluid, which lubricates the joint. Without cartilage and fluid, your bones would grind against each other when you moved. If you force a joint beyond the limits of the ligaments, they may tear. This is a *sprain*. If the bones slip out of place, they are said to be *dislocated*.

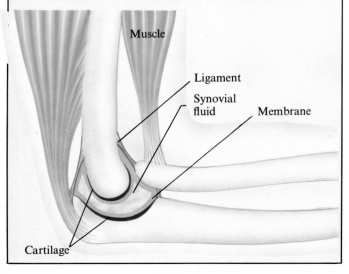

Muscle

Ligament

Synovial fluid

Membrane

Cartilage

Muscles and Movement

Most animals move from place to place to find food, water, a mate or to escape from danger. Even one-celled animals respond to changes in their environment by making simple movements backward and forward. They are able to do this because parts of the cell have the power to contract (shorten). More complex animals, such as fish, birds and mammals, act in the same way but have highly developed muscles which help them to carry out more precise movements, such as running, swimming and flying. Did you realize that almost all the meat we eat is muscle?

Animals with outside skeletons, such as insects, have their muscles attached to the inside of their skeletons. But they work in a similar way to your muscles. Animals with inside skeletons have muscles attached to the outside of the bones that make up their skeleton. You have over 600 muscles, many of which are arranged in layers over your skeleton.

Some of your muscles (such as those in your arms and legs) work when you want them to. They are called *voluntary muscles*. But other muscles (such as those in your stomach) work automatically, without your being aware of them. They are called *involuntary muscles*. A ring of involuntary muscle (called a *sphincter*) opens or closes the entrance or exit to a hollow organ, such as the stomach. A third type of muscle, called *cardiac muscle*, is what a heart is

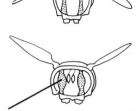

When these muscles contract, the wings go down.

When these muscles contract, the wings go up.

Above: A honeybee in flight. Insect flight muscles are attached to the thorax (the middle part of the body) rather than to the wings themselves. By contracting and relaxing these muscles, they can move their wings rapidly.

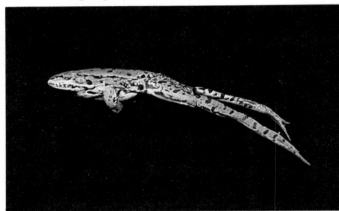

Above: Powerful muscles in the back legs of this edible frog thrust it into the air. The smaller front legs help the frog to steer when it is swimming and absorb the shock of landing after a jump on land.

Below: The cheetah's long legs and flexible spine make it the fastest animal over short distances. It has a top speed of over 68 miles per hour (110 kilometers per hour) and can reach about 43 miles per hour (70 kilometers per hour) in just two seconds. But cheetahs cannot keep up such high speeds for long because their body temperature rises dangerously high and would damage the brain. They use up so much energy when they chase animals that they may have to rest for up to 15 minutes after a fast sprint.

A cheetah chasing a herd of impala on the African savanna.

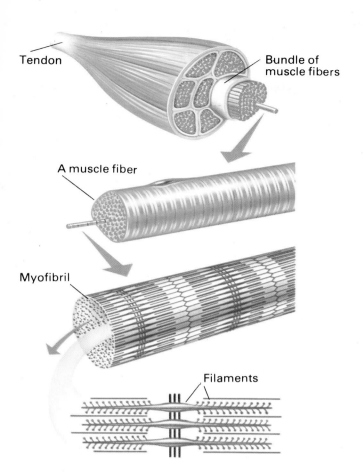

Tendon

Bundle of muscle fibers

A muscle fiber

Myofibril

Filaments

Above: The fibers in a voluntary muscle are made up of strands called myofibrils. And each myofibril is made up of two kinds of tiny interlocking filaments. When these filaments overlap, the muscle fibers become shorter and the muscle contracts. The filaments are held in place by chemical links. When they move apart, the muscle relaxes. Each muscle fiber can either contract completely or not at all. But not all the fibers in a muscle have to contract at once, so the pulling power of a muscle can vary.

Below: A striated (striped) muscle from a mammal under a microscope. The stripes are caused by the two different proteins, actin and myosin, which make up the filaments in the myofibrils.

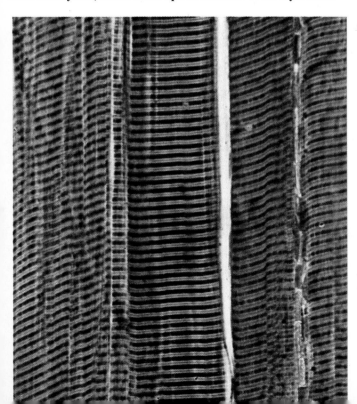

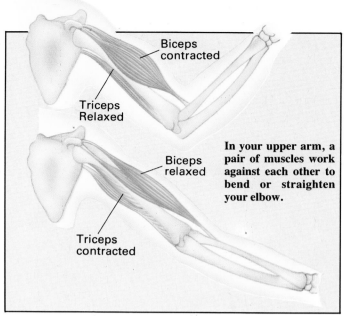

Biceps contracted

Triceps Relaxed

Biceps relaxed

In your upper arm, a pair of muscles work against each other to bend or straighten your elbow.

Triceps contracted

made of. It works automatically and will continue to make the heart beat even after it has been removed.

Inside a Muscle

A muscle is made of bundles of long, thin cells called muscle fibers. The bundles are held together by and enclosed within *connective tissues*. You can see how the fibers of voluntary muscle are arranged in the diagram to the left. It is called *striped muscle* because of its appearance under the microscope. Involuntary muscle has no stripes, so it is called *smooth muscle*. Cardiac muscle is in between the two. It has some stripes but fewer of them and the fibers are branched.

How Does a Muscle Work?

Voluntary muscles contract (get shorter) when they receive electrical impulses from nerves and relax (get longer) when they do not. This means they can only pull, they cannot push. So most muscles work in pairs, one pulling one way, the other pulling the opposite way. They are called *antagonistic* muscles, which means they work against each other.

Muscles convert food and oxygen to pulling power. But this produces harmful waste products, such as lactic acid. If these waste products build up, it stops nerve impulses reaching the muscles and they "feel tired." The drug curare has the same effect. South American indians used to cover their arrow–heads with it for hunting – some still do. If the prey is not killed by the arrow, it will be paralyzed by the curare.

33

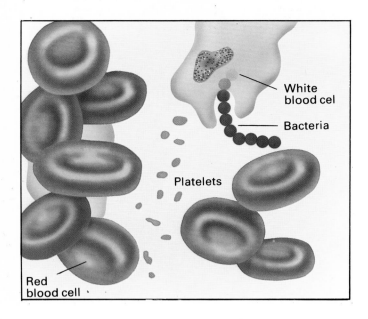

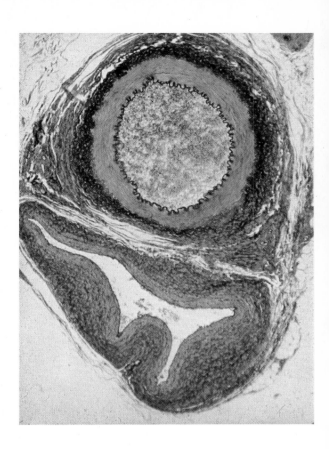

Above: Your blood is made of red and white blood cells and platelets floating in a liquid called plasma. One drop of blood contains about 5,000,000 red cells and 5,000 white cells. The body of an average-sized adult contains about 8-10 pints (5-6 liters) of blood.

Right: Section through an artery (top) and a vein. Arteries have thick elastic walls because blood pulses through them at high pressure.

Blood — a Transport System

Blood is far more than a red liquid that carries oxygen. It is a transport system for food, waste products and hormones (see page 49). It carries a chemical repair kit in case of injury, and defenses to protect animals against infections and poisons. In mammals and birds it helps to keep the body at a constant temperature.

What is Your Blood Made of?
Your blood is made of a mixture of cells floating in a straw-colored liquid called *plasma*. Plasma is 90 percent water and contains dissolved nutrients, vitamins, minerals, proteins and wastes. Red blood cells carry oxygen from the lungs to all parts of the body. They can do this because they contain a complex protein molecule called *hemoglobin*. This takes in oxygen where there is a high concentration, such as in the lungs. It then becomes *oxyhemoglobin*, which is bright red. Where the concentration of oxygen is low (where cells are using up oxygen in their life processes) oxyhemoglobin releases its oxygen to become hemoglobin again.

You have an incredible number of red blood cells. A teaspoon of blood contains about 25 million cells. They live for about four months and are finally broken up in the liver or spleen. New blood cells have to be made in your bone marrow because mature red cells have no nucleus and cannot reproduce themselves. About one percent of your red blood cells are replaced every day.

The other inhabitants of the blood are the white cells. There is only one white cell for every 500 to 1000 red cells. They are made in the bone marrow, lymph nodes and spleen. One kind of white cell, called a *granulocyte*, helps to fight infections by eating harmful bacteria. It also removes wastes and dead cells. Another kind of white cell, called a *lymphocyte*, detects anything alien in the blood or lymph (see page 37) and causes antibodies to be produced to destroy or neutralize the invaders. This is what happens when an organ is transplanted from another person's body. Powerful drugs have to be taken to stop the antibodies destroying the organ.

Blood *platelets* are tiny fragments of large cells in your bone marrow. Their purpose is to clump together to help form blood clots, which stop wounds bleeding and seal them against bacteria.

Pipelines for Blood

Blood travels around your body in tubes called *blood vessels*. It is pumped by the heart to all parts of the body along thousands of miles of blood vessels. Red blood cells travel around the body in less than a minute. All vessels carrying blood *from* the heart are called *arteries*. All vessels carrying blood *to* the heart are called *veins*. Arteries and veins are linked by a network of microscopic vessels called *capillaries*, which pass between the cells of all the tissues in your body.

Arteries are tough, muscular vessels. They have to be thick-walled to withstand the pressure of blood coming straight from the heart. In veins, the blood flows slower and at a lower pressure than in arteries, so the walls of veins are thinner and have valves to stop the blood flowing backward. Blood in veins has given up its oxygen and lost its red color. You can see this if you look at the veins in your wrist.

Capillaries are very narrow vessels with thin walls only one cell thick. They are only just wide enough for red blood cells to pass along, so blood flows very slowly through them. This (together with the thin walls) helps substances such as food and oxygen to pass into the tissue fluid, and waste products to pass back into the capillaries. The tissue fluid carries the substances into the individual cells. In this way, the capillaries deliver to and collect from all parts of the body.

Right: This diagram shows the main blood vessels in the human body. Arteries (shown in red) carry food and oxygen from the heart to the organs and limbs. Veins (shown in blue) carry the blood back to the heart. Blood circulates continuously around the body, driven by the pumping of the heart.

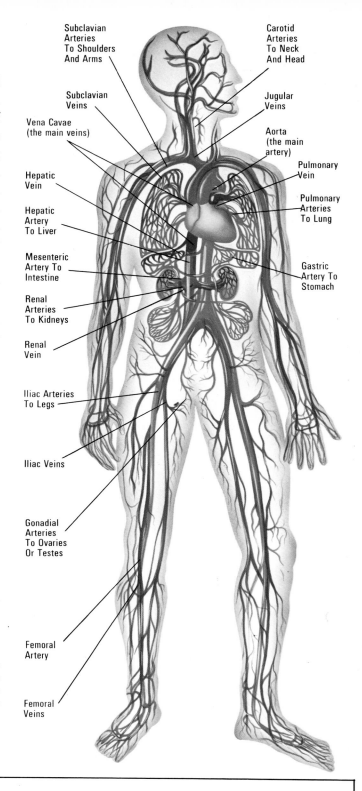

Subclavian Arteries To Shoulders And Arms

Carotid Arteries To Neck And Head

Subclavian Veins

Jugular Veins

Vena Cavae (the main veins)

Aorta (the main artery)

Hepatic Vein

Pulmonary Vein

Pulmonary Arteries To Lung

Hepatic Artery To Liver

Mesenteric Artery To Intestine

Gastric Artery To Stomach

Renal Arteries To Kidneys

Renal Vein

Iliac Arteries To Legs

Iliac Veins

Gonadial Arteries To Ovaries Or Testes

Femoral Artery

Femoral Veins

STOPPING LEAKS

1. When blood vessels are damaged, tiny platelets gather around the wound. They give off an enzyme that helps sticky threads of fibrin to develop.

2. The threads form a web that traps red blood cells and platelets. This thickens to form a scab, which stops bleeding and keeps bacteria out.

3. New skin grows beneath the scab. People suffering from hemophilia do not have one of the substances needed for blood clotting, and could die from even small cuts.

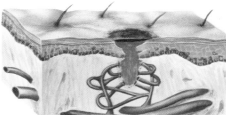

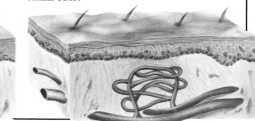

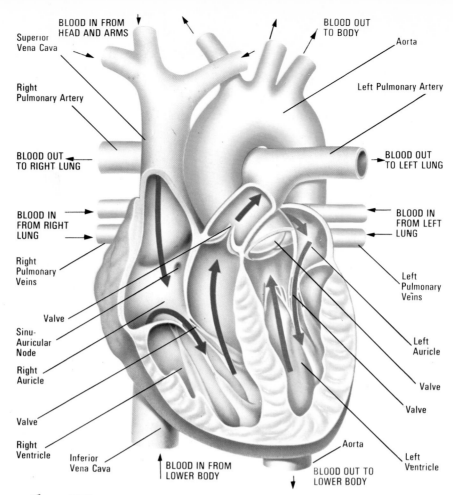

Superior Vena Cava

BLOOD IN FROM HEAD AND ARMS

Right Pulmonary Artery

BLOOD OUT TO RIGHT LUNG

BLOOD IN FROM RIGHT LUNG

Right Pulmonary Veins

Valve

Sinu-Auricular Node

Right Auricle

Valve

Right Ventricle

Inferior Vena Cava

BLOOD IN FROM LOWER BODY

BLOOD OUT TO BODY

Aorta

Left Pulmonary Artery

BLOOD OUT TO LEFT LUNG

BLOOD IN FROM LEFT LUNG

Left Pulmonary Veins

Left Auricle

Valve

Valve

Aorta

Left Ventricle

BLOOD OUT TO LOWER BODY

The Body Pump

The human heart is a very strong and specialized muscle about the size of a person's fist. The job of the heart is to pump enough blood at a high enough pressure so that it travels throughout the body and returns to the heart. The whole circuit takes about 45 seconds.

The heart has four chambers – the two at the top are called *atria* (singular *atrium*) and the two at the bottom are called *ventricles*. The atrium and ventricle on the right side pump blood to the lungs to get rid of waste carbon dioxide and pick up fresh oxygen. The atrium and ventricle on the left side pump oxygen-rich blood to all parts of the body. As the heart pumps, four valves open and close to prevent the blood from flowing backward.

How Does the Heart Work?
Blood returning from its journey around the body flows into the *vena cava*, which leads into the right atrium. Then it passes through a valve into the right ventricle. The right ventricle then contracts, pumping the blood through a second valve into the *pulmonary artery*, which leads to the lungs. Here carbon dioxide is released from the blood and oxygen taken up.

The blood flows back to the left atrium of the heart through the *pulmonary veins*. From the left atrium, it passes through a third valve into the left ventricle. This then contracts and oxygen-rich blood is pumped out at high pressure through a fourth valve into the *aorta* – the main artery of the body. Both atria contract at the same time, as do both ventricles. The complete cycle usually takes less than one second.

The heart beat is a characteristic of heart muscle, with nerves helping to maintain a steady beat at the right pace. The heart of an average adult beats about 70 times a minute. Athletes develop more powerful hearts through years of exercise. They can pump more blood with every beat so their heart beat is usually slower. Many top athletes have heart rates below 50. The heart rate of birds is much higher than that of human beings because birds need a lot of energy to fly. A sparrow has a heart rate of about 500 beats a minute.

HEARTS AND CIRCULATION

All vertebrates and some invertebrates have a transport system of blood vessels containing blood, which is moved around the body either by muscles contracting in the vessel walls or by the pumping action of a heart. A heart is really an expanded blood vessel with a thick muscular wall. In fish, the heart has two chambers, in many reptiles and amphibians it has three chambers and in mammals and birds it has four chambers. In a four-chambered heart, oxygen-rich blood can be separated from oxygen-poor blood for more efficient use.

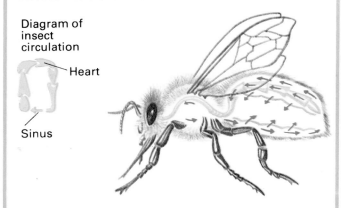

Diagram of insect circulation

Heart

Sinus

Above: Insect blood is contained in an open space called a *sinus*, rather than in blood vessels. It is kept moving by the heart, which sucks in blood through little holes in its sides and pumps it out through a hole at the front. Insect blood is a colorless fluid, which carries food and waste substances, but not oxygen (see page 43).

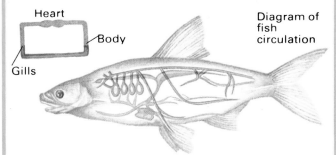

Heart

Body

Gills

Diagram of fish circulation

Above: A fish heart has only one atrium and one ventricle. It pumps oxygen-poor blood from the body to the gills, where it takes up oxygen. Oxygen-rich blood then flows to various parts of the body where oxygen is needed, before eventually returning to the heart.

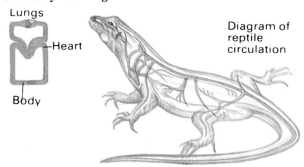

Lungs

Heart

Body

Diagram of reptile circulation

Above: In most reptiles, the heart has two atria but the ventricle is only partly divided. When the ventricle pumps blood, some goes to the lungs and the rest goes to all the other cells in the body. Oxygen-poor blood seems to go mainly to the lungs and oxygen-rich blood goes mainly to the tissues.

THE LYMPH SYSTEM

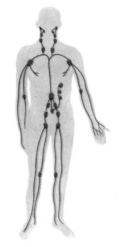

Left: The main lymph vessels (shown in red) and lymph nodes (shown in blue) in a human.

Below: Lymph nodes range in size from that of a pinhead to that of a broad bean. Many nodes are grouped in the floor and roof of the mouth (tonsils and adenoids) and in the neck, armpits and groin. When the nodes are fighting an infection, they become enlarged and tender. Then you may have a sore throat or infected tonsils.

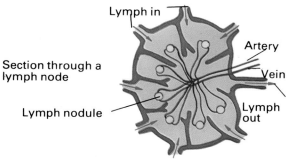

Lymph in

Artery

Vein

Lymph out

Section through a lymph node

Lymph nodule

Your Lymph System

Along with your blood system, there is another transport system in the body, the *lymph* network. Inside the lymph vessels is a colorless fluid called lymph, which is similar to blood without the red cells. It comes from excess fluids that leak out of your capillaries into the spaces between your cells. Lymph fluid flows eventually into your bloodstream when the lymph vessels join major veins which lead directly to the heart.

The lymph system has no pump. Exercise and pressure move lymph forward and valves stop any backflow. Lymph vessels also collect fats directly from the small intestine (the *ileum*) and transport them to your cells. At various points along the lymph vessels are lymph nodes. They filter out and destroy bacteria in the lymph and make white blood cells called *lymphocytes*.

Lymphocytes produce *antibodies*, which seek out alien bodies, such as viruses or bacteria, and make them harmless. They detect invaders by their various proteins, which are different from the proteins of the body itself. You are able to produce up to a million different antibodies.

Food, Teeth and Diet

Food does two main things for an animal. It provides energy for the work the cells do, and raw materials for building, repairing and controlling body tissues. All animals feed on either plants or other animals or a mixture of both – as you do. They are equipped with the teeth (or mouthparts) and digestive systems to cope with their particular diet.

A few animals get all the nutrients they need from only one type of food. Koalas eat nothing but the leaves of certain eucalyptus trees, a diet that would poison other animals. Animals with specialized diets have specialized digestive systems. Even cows, sheep and other grazing animals need specialized digestive systems to get enough nourishment from the large amounts of cellulose (a tough material) in grass and other plants. They have a large *cecum* and *appendix* which contain vast numbers of bacteria that digest cellulose for them. (A *cecum* is a blindly-ending piece of gut at the junction of the small and large intestines. The *appendix* is an extension of this.)

Teeth are a good indication of what an animal eats. Plant-eaters, especially grazing animals, have flat teeth with ridges on the surface for grinding up their rough diet. Meat-eaters have long, sharp teeth to kill and tear the flesh of their prey. Human beings have very unspecialized teeth, which would indicate to a biologist from another planet that they eat a wide variety of foods. But we need a balanced diet to keep us healthy.

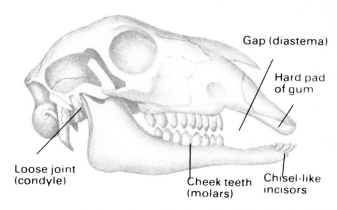

Above: The skull of a sheep, showing the teeth of a typical plant-eater. Sheep have no canine teeth and there is a toothless gap between their front teeth (the incisors) and their back teeth (the molars). Sheep have loose joints between the lower jaw and the skull so they can move their lower jaw from side to side when they chew. This helps the grinding action of the cheek teeth.

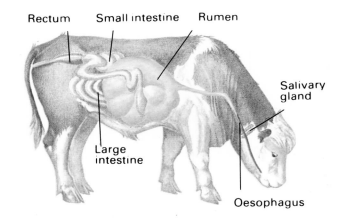

Above: The digestive system of a cow. The intestine can be as long as 12 feet (40 meters). This slows down digestion so that tough plant material can be broken down before it reaches the end of the gut. A cow's stomach has four chambers, the first of which is called the *rumen*. The cow eats grass and swallows it into the rumen without chewing it first. After a while, it coughs up (regurgitates) the food and chews it in the mouth. This helps digestion and is called *chewing the cud*.

The teeth on the *radula* (a tongue-like structure) of a snail under a high-power microscope. The radula is used to rasp tissue from plants.

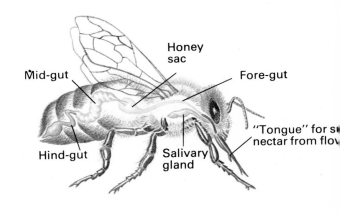

Above: The digestive system of a honeybee. The gut is divided into three parts, the fore-gut, the mid-gut and the hind-gut. Food is pushed through the gut by *peristalsis* (see page 40).

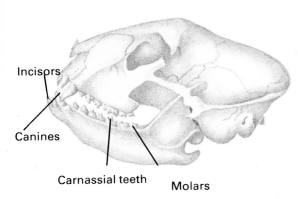

Above: Meat-eaters have dagger-like *canines* to kill their prey and tear its flesh. Their sharp cheek teeth slide past each other to slice off flesh and crack bones. The back teeth (*molars*) have more flattened surfaces and meet together to crush the food into smaller particles. The jaws are very powerful and the lower jaw only moves up and down. This helps to prevent the jaw from being dislocated.

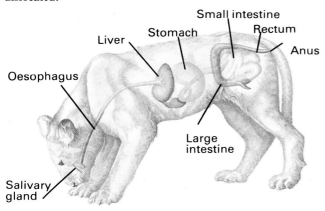

Above: The digestive system of a lion. Most digestion takes place in the small intestine, where enzymes complete the breakdown of food begun in the mouth and stomach. When digestion is completed, the finger-like *villi* that line the walls of the small intestine, pick up nutrients. The nutrients pass through the thin walls of the villi into the blood and are carried around the body to all the cells that need energy.

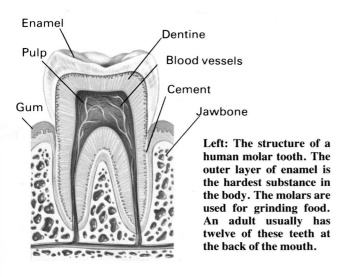

Left: The structure of a human molar tooth. The outer layer of enamel is the hardest substance in the body. The molars are used for grinding food. An adult usually has twelve of these teeth at the back of the mouth.

Different Kinds of Food

Scientists classify foods as proteins, carbohydrates, fats, vitamins, minerals and roughage. Water is also a major part of food – you are about 60 percent water.

Proteins are essential for the growth and repair of animal tissues. They are formed from about twenty basic units called *amino acids*. These link together to form chains, which fold up in many ways to form a huge variety of protein molecules. The main sources of protein in your diet are meat, fish, eggs and dairy products. Beans and peas are also a good and cheap source of protein.

Carbohydrates usually provide the body's main energy requirements. They include sugars and starch.

Fats are essential to the life of every cell. They supply twice as much energy as other foods and some are used in the formation of cell membranes. Some fat may be used immediately and the rest is stored as body fat. The main sources of fat are milk, vegetable oil, eggs and meat fat.

Tiny quantities of *vitamins* are needed to keep the chemical processes in an animal's body working efficiently. For example, you need vitamin D for strong bones and teeth and vitamin A to see in dim light. People have to take in their vitamins ready-made. We cannot make vitamin C in our bodies. We get it through eating fruits and vegetables. But cats, which do not get vitamin C in this way, can make their own.

Minerals carry out vital roles in an animal's body. For example, you need iron for red blood cells, calcium, magnesium and phosphorus for bones and teeth and sodium and potassium for your nerves and muscles.

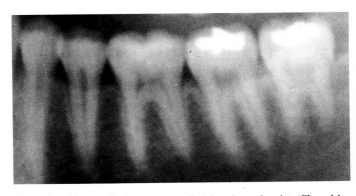

Part of an X-ray of a human mouth taken by a dentist. The white patches are fillings in the molar teeth. You can see the pulp cavity in the middle of these teeth.

39

Food Pathways

Before food can be used by your cells, it has to be broken down into a form the blood can carry. This process is called *digestion*.

In the mouth, your teeth bite and chew the food into small pieces. Salivary glands under the tongue produce *saliva*, which helps to bind the food particles together and make the food easier to swallow. Saliva contains the first digestive enzyme, which starts to break down starch. (*Enzymes* speed up chemical reactions in the body but are not changed themselves in the reaction. So they can be used over and over again. Each enzyme works only in a particular reaction.) As you swallow, a flap of skin called the *epiglottis* blocks off the windpipe so the food goes down the right hole. It reaches the stomach in about six seconds.

The stomach mixes up the food and adds digestive juices, which include the enzyme *pepsin*. This starts to digest proteins. A normal meal may remain in the stomach for two to four hours before it is pushed into the duodenum, the first part of the small intestine.

In the *duodenum*, food is mixed with bile from the liver, which is stored in the gall bladder. Bile breaks up fats so that *enzymes* can work on them. Juices from the pancreas are also poured into the duodenum. These contain a range of enzymes, such as *trypsin* and *amylase*, which help to complete the breakdown of all types of food. By the time the food gets to the *ileum*, most of it has been digested. It passes through the walls of the ileum into the blood. (Fats go into lymph vessels and enter the blood later.)

Your blood carries the digested food to your *liver* for more processing before taking it to all the body's tissues. Undigested food (mainly fiber) and water pass into the large intestine. Although there are no enzymes in the large intestine, the bacteria that live there break down some of the remaining matter as they feed. Most of the water passes into your blood through the walls of the first part of the large intestine – the *colon*. More solid waste is stored further along in the *rectum* and pushed out of the body as feces.

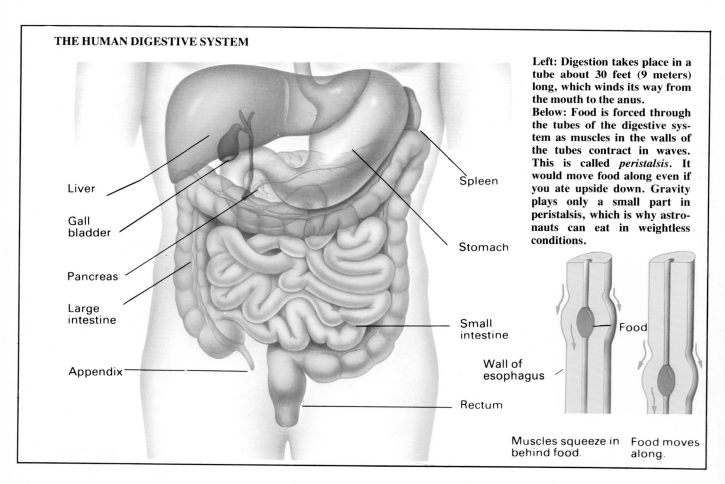

THE HUMAN DIGESTIVE SYSTEM

Liver

Gall bladder

Pancreas

Large intestine

Appendix

Spleen

Stomach

Small intestine

Wall of esophagus

Rectum

Left: Digestion takes place in a tube about 30 feet (9 meters) long, which winds its way from the mouth to the anus.
Below: Food is forced through the tubes of the digestive system as muscles in the walls of the tubes contract in waves. This is called *peristalsis*. It would move food along even if you ate upside down. Gravity plays only a small part in peristalsis, which is why astronauts can eat in weightless conditions.

Food

Muscles squeeze in behind food.

Food moves along.

Getting Rid of Wastes

Animal cells and tissues constantly produce chemical wastes that will poison them if they are not removed. This removal process is called *excretion* and the main organs of excretion are the kidneys. (The lungs, liver and sweat glands in the skin also help the body to remove waste substances.)

Your kidneys are at the back of your abdomen, roughly on a level with your waist. They work by filtering substances out of the blood and then taking back the substances the body needs, such as water and salts. Blood flows to the kidneys through renal arteries, and filtered blood returns to the body via the renal veins, which join the vena cava.

The fluid and waste substances filtered out by the kidneys, which is called *urine*, passes down two tubes called *ureters* into your bladder. The bladder is a muscular bag with a tight band of muscle, called a sphincter, holding it shut. When you relax the sphincter, the muscles in the wall of your bladder contract and the urine flows into a tube called a *urethra* and out of your body.

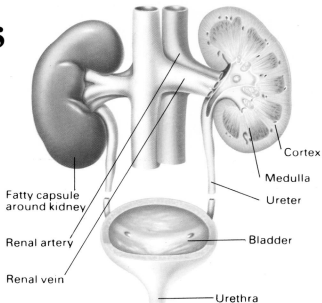

Above: The human excretory system. The kidney to the right of the picture has been cross-sectioned to reveal the darker outer part (the cortex) and the lighter inner part (the medulla). The cortex contains a network of fine blood vessels that branch from the renal artery. Each one of these ends as a little bunch of capillaries called the glomerulus, where blood is filtered.

Right: One of the millions of filtering units in a human kidney. The pressure of blood in the *glomerulus* forces the fluid part of the blood through the walls of the capillaries into the space inside the capsule. The fluid that goes through contains urea, glucose, water and salt. (*Urea* is a waste substance produced during the breakdown of amino acids – the units proteins are made of.) The fluid goes into the tubule, where all the glucose and amino acids, and almost all the water and salts, are taken back into the capillaries wrapped around the tubule. The rest of the fluid, which consists mainly of water, salts and urea, passes into the ureter as urine.

Below: A microscopic view of a *glomerulus*, part of a filtering unit in a mammal's kidney.

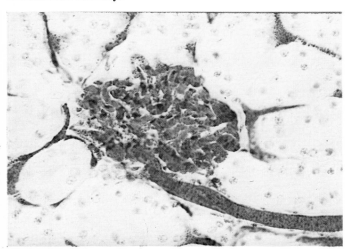

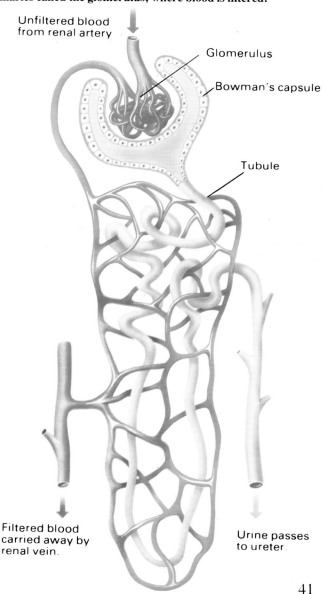

41

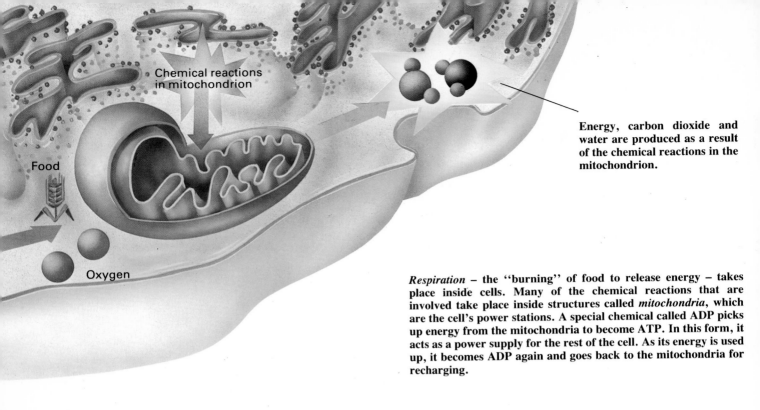

Chemical reactions
in mitochondrion

Food

Oxygen

Energy, carbon dioxide and water are produced as a result of the chemical reactions in the mitochondrion.

Respiration – the "burning" of food to release energy – takes place inside cells. Many of the chemical reactions that are involved take place inside structures called *mitochondria*, which are the cell's power stations. A special chemical called ADP picks up energy from the mitochondria to become ATP. In this form, it acts as a power supply for the rest of the cell. As its energy is used up, it becomes ADP again and goes back to the mitochondria for recharging.

Energy from Food

All animals "burn" food inside their cells to provide the energy they need to keep their bodies working. This process is called *respiration* and involves combining food with oxygen in a series of chemical reactions, which are controlled by enzymes. Energy is released from the food, while carbon dioxide and water are produced as by-products.

Animals obtain oxygen in a variety of ways. Microscopic single-celled animals have no problem because they are so small. They have a large surface area compared to the volume of their bodies and all the oxygen they need passes through their cell membrane. Some many-celled animals get their oxygen in a similar way. Tadpoles do so in their early stages of development and an adult frog absorbs enough oxygen through its skin to keep it alive at the bottom of a pond during a winter's hibernation.

Insects have a system of tubes called *tracheae* (singular *trachea*) to allow oxygen to reach all their body tissues. Air enters an insect's body through holes called *spiracles*, which are opened or closed by valves. Each spiracle leads to a tracheal tube, which branches and becomes thinner and thinner until it ends up as a network of tiny tubes called *tracheoles*. These contain the membranes through which oxygen passes into an insect's cells.

The ends of the tracheoles are filled with fluid that keeps the membranes moist. This helps oxygen to pass through because gases must dissolve in fluid before they can enter cells. Most insects do not push air through the tracheae. But large and active insects, such as the locust, use muscles in their abdomen to pump air through. This allows them to release a lot of energy from their food.

Large animals cannot get their oxygen like insects because it would take too long for the oxygen to reach all their tissues. Instead they transport oxygen in their blood and have special organs such as *gills* and *lungs* to absorb oxygen.

Gills are the breathing organs of most animals that live underwater. Gills have a large surface area and a lot of blood vessels beneath thin protective membranes. Oxygen passes through the membranes and the walls of the blood vessels into the bloodstream. Carbon dioxide passes out in the opposite direction.

Most fish have gills to take in oxygen from the water. They take in water through their mouths and force it over their gills. (Not all animals with gills do this. The lobster bales water past its gills.) A few fish also have lungs – they are called lungfish. Their lungs are a backup system, which helps them to get oxygen when the rivers they live in dry up.

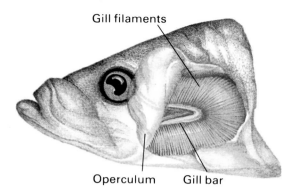

Gill filaments

Operculum   Gill bar

HOW A DOGFISH BREATHES IN

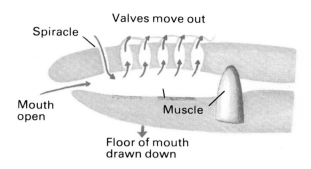

Valves move out

Spiracle

Mouth open

Muscle

Floor of mouth drawn down

HOW A DOGFISH BREATHES OUT

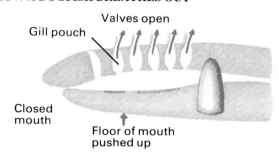

Valves open

Gill pouch

Closed mouth

Floor of mouth pushed up

A fish uses its gills for breathing and needs to keep a continuous stream of water flowing over them. Some fish pump water over their gills. Bony fish do this by opening and closing the operculum (a muscular flap of skin that covers the gills) and opening and closing the mouth. Cartilagenous fish, such as the dogfish, have flaplike branchial valves instead of an operculum. These open and close to draw water over the gills in the same way. Fast-swimming fish swim with their mouths open, which forces water over the gills.

Above: Two diagrams to show how a dogfish draws water past its gills. To breathe in, it opens its mouth and pulls the floor of the mouth and pharynx down. This draws water into the mouth. The flaplike valves covering the gills move outward to draw water past the gills. To breathe out, the dogfish closes its mouth and pushes up the floor of the mouth and pharynx. The valves open and water is sucked out over the gills where oxygen is absorbed from the water and carbon dioxide is given out.

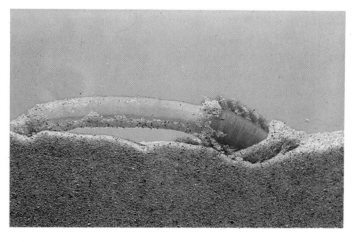

Left: The feathery gills of this lugworm show up along the side of its body. The lugworm burrows in mud and sand on the seabed, where there is very little oxygen. The hemoglobin in its blood is able to pick up oxygen even when it is present in very small amounts.

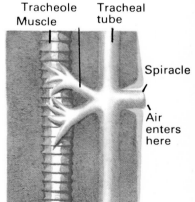

Tracheole   Tracheal tube

Muscle

Spiracle

Air enters here

Below: These pond dwellers obtain the oxygen they need in a variety of ways. Some water snails come to the surface to fill their lungs. Backswimmers and water beetles also collect air from the surface but store it as bubbles under their wing cases. Drone fly larvae and water scorpions draw in air from the surface through long breathing tubes – just as people do when they use a snorkel. Mosquito larvae also have a breathing tube at the back end of their body. The end of the tube is open so air can get in. Look out for these larvae hanging from the surface of the water in ponds during the summer. The only truly underwater creature in this picture is the mayfly nymph, which has gills to take oxygen from the water. The gills look like three long tails.

Right: A small part of the breathing tubes (*tracheae*) of an insect. Holes called *spiracles* lead into two main tracheae along each side of the body. Smaller tubes called *tracheoles*, branch out from these to reach all the tissues of the body. Gases are exchanged at the end of each tracheole.

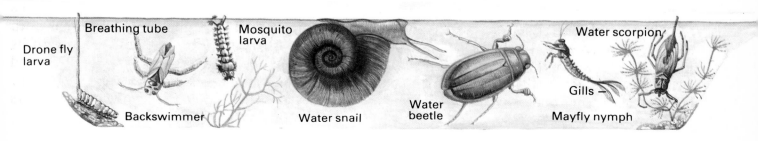

Drone fly larva   Breathing tube   Mosquito larva   Water scorpion

Backswimmer   Water snail   Water beetle   Gills   Mayfly nymph

The Breath of Life

Oxygen enters your body in the air you breathe into your lungs. There it moves into the bloodstream and is carried to all your body cells where it is used in the chemical reactions that release energy from food. The waste gas produced in this process, carbon dioxide, moves from the blood into the air in your lungs and leaves the body as you breathe out.

You usually breathe automatically at a rate of about 16 breaths a minute – try timing yourself. If you hold your breath, the amount of carbon dioxide in the blood builds up. This is detected by the brain and if the amount gets dangerously high, it sends out signals which make you breathe. This is one of the many feedback systems that work to keep your body running smoothly.

Where are Your Lungs?

Your lungs fill most of the chest cavity, which is an airtight box formed by the ribs, sternum, backbone and diaphragm. Each lung is surrounded by two thin sheets of tissue called the *pleural membranes*. The inner one covers the lungs and the outer one lines the inside of the chest cavity. Between the two is a narrow space containing a fluid. This makes the membranes slippery so they slide over each other smoothly as you breathe in and out.

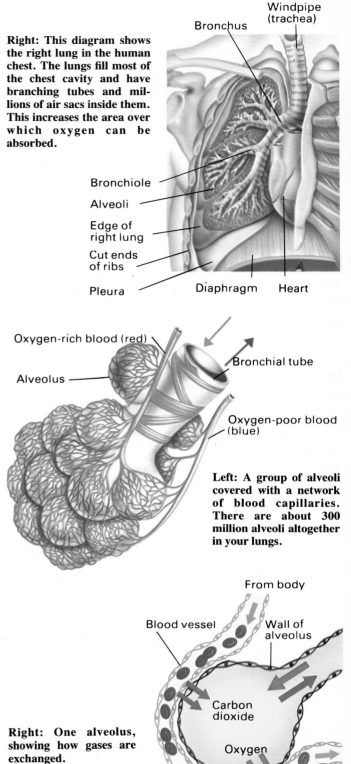

Right: This diagram shows the right lung in the human chest. The lungs fill most of the chest cavity and have branching tubes and millions of air sacs inside them. This increases the area over which oxygen can be absorbed.

Windpipe (trachea)
Bronchus
Bronchiole
Alveoli
Edge of right lung
Cut ends of ribs
Pleura
Diaphragm
Heart

Oxygen-rich blood (red)
Alveolus
Bronchial tube
Oxygen-poor blood (blue)

Left: A group of alveoli covered with a network of blood capillaries. There are about 300 million alveoli altogether in your lungs.

From body
Blood vessel
Wall of alveolus
Carbon dioxide
Oxygen
To body
Red blood cells

Right: One alveolus, showing how gases are exchanged.

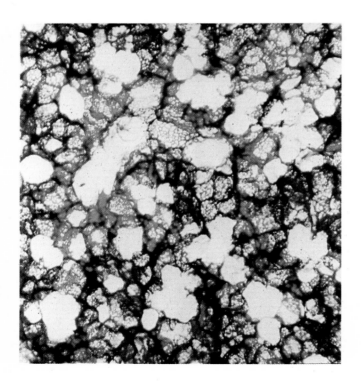

Above: Each alveolus has a wall only one cell thick. Oxygen from the air passes into the blood vessels and carbon dioxide moves from the blood into the alveolus.
Left: Lung tissue under the microscope, showing some of the *alveoli* (air sacs) with blood vessels around them.

How You Breathe

Breathing is controlled by the movements of muscles in your chest, which suck air in and force it out. When you breathe in, your rib cage is pulled upward by your chest muscles. At the same time, the diaphragm is lowered. These two movements expand the space in your lungs, making the air pressure inside your body lower than it is outside. Air rushes in to fill the space. These actions happen in reverse when you breathe out. Most people have room for about 7 to 9 pints (4 to 5 liters) of air in their lungs but they only exchange about a pint (half a liter) of air on each breath.

Pathways for Air

When the lungs are expanded, air is sucked through your nose or mouth and down the windpipe (*trachea*). The trachea branches into two tubes called *bronchi* (singular *bronchus*), one entering each lung. Within each lung, the bronchus splits into many branches like a tree. The branches are called *bronchioles*.

Each bronchiole leads into a bunch of tiny sacs called *alveoli* (singular *alveolus*). There are about 350 million alveoli in a pair of lungs. They are surrounded by a network of blood capillaries and have very thin membranes (just one cell thick) so that oxygen, carbon dioxide and water can pass easily through them.

The trachea and bronchi are reinforced with rings of cartilage. This prevents them from collapsing when you breathe out. They are also lined with goblet cells which produce a slippery

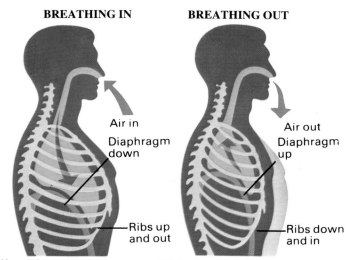

BREATHING IN

Air in
Diaphragm down

Ribs up and out

BREATHING OUT

Air out
Diaphragm up

Ribs down and in

liquid called mucus. This helps to trap dust particles and germs that have escaped being caught in the nose passages. Tiny hairs called *cilia* gently waft the mucus away from your lungs towards your nose and throat so it can be swallowed or coughed and sneezed out.

How Much Oxygen?

The energy released when food is "burned" in our cells is measured in *calories* – a measure of the energy the food contains. The average person at rest uses 1.2 calories a minute and this consumes about 15 cubic inches (250 cubic centimeters) of oxygen. An active man will use up about 3,000 calories a day. A woman uses slightly less. A person may use thirty times more oxygen during exercise.

How Birds Breathe

Birds have a very efficient system of respiration to provide the extra energy they need for flight. They have special air sacs as well as lungs. When a bird breathes in, its blood gets oxygen once as air passes through the lungs into the air sacs. As in other animals, only some of the oxygen in this air passes into the blood. Then, as the bird breathes out, the air travels back through the lungs and is used again. So one breath provides two helpings of oxygen. The air in the air sacs also makes the bird lighter (which helps it to fly) and helps to cool its body.

Bird blood cells carry a large amount of oxygen and very large arteries supply blood to the flight muscles. The hearts of birds beat faster to pump blood around the body as quickly as possible. Small, active birds may eat a third of their body weight each day to provide enough energy to meet their high energy needs.

A view inside a goose to show the air sacs, which are linked to each bronchus by tubes inside the lungs.

Trachea

Air sac

45

A Communications Network

All animals react to their surroundings and in most animals these reactions depend on electrical signals (*nerve impulses*) sent around the body by nerve cells. Nerve cells are usually linked together to form a communications network, which collects information and sends out instructions to control the way an animal's body works.

Invertebrates, such as hydra, have the simplest sort of nervous system. It is made up of a net of nerve cells, which reaches all over its body. More complex invertebrates, such as worms, have bunches of nerves called *ganglia* as well as a nerve net. The ganglia are like simple brains. Of all the invertebrates, the octopuses and squid have a nervous system and brain most similar to ours. They even have a cranium of cartilage to protect their brain, just as the human brain is protected by the bones of the skull.

All vertebrates have complex nervous systems. The brain and the spinal cord (inside the backbone) together are called the *central nervous system*. From the central nervous system, bundles of nerve cells branch out to all parts of the body. One of the most remarkable events in the history of life is the evolution of very large brains, especially in people.

Nerves and How they Work

The basic unit of all nervous systems is the nerve cell. A typical nerve cell has a cell body with short branches called *dendrites* all around it and a much longer branch, called an *axon*, extending from one side. Axons can be up to three feet (a meter) long – you have some that reach from your toes to your spinal cord.

What people call a "nerve" is really a bundle of axons surrounded by a protective sheath of fatty material called *myelin*. This stops nerve impulses escaping and helps them to travel faster. The thickest myelin-covered nerves can send impulses at 450 feet (150 meters) per second. Uncovered nerves can manage a speed of only three feet (one meter) a second. Nerves are rather like the telephone wires between your phone and the telephone company switchboard.

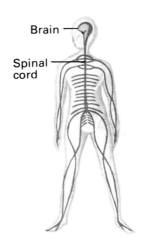

Brain

Spinal cord

This is a simplified diagram of your nervous system, showing how nerves reach to all parts of the body. Each nerve is made up of a bundle of nerve fibers. Each fiber is part of a nerve cell. The brain and the spinal cord are called the *central nervous system*.

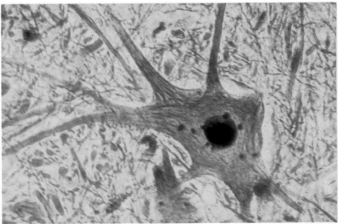

Above: The cell body of a motor nerve cell from the spinal cord under a high-power microscope.
Below: The nervous systems of three invertebrates.

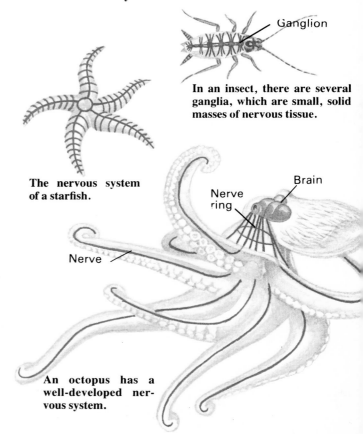

Ganglion

In an insect, there are several ganglia, which are small, solid masses of nervous tissue.

The nervous system of a starfish.

Brain

Nerve ring

Nerve

An octopus has a well-developed nervous system.

Instant Action

Most of the movements of animals, especially in emergencies, are automatic. They have to be to prevent injury or even death. For instance, if you put your hand on something hot, it will be pulled away immediately. In such emergencies, the message from the sensory nerves in the skin does not travel to the brain for instructions. Instead, nerves in your spinal cord instruct the muscles to move your hand. This is called an *automatic reflex action*. All animals are armed with a wide range of reflex actions, such as coughing and sneezing. The way the pupils in your eyes contract in bright light is also a reflex action.

Animals can also be trained to carry out automatic reflex actions. These are called *conditioned reflexes*. For example, in a series of experiments, the Russian doctor Ivan Pavlov rang a bell before he gave food to a dog. An automatic reflex makes dogs produce saliva when they see food. After a while the dog produced saliva when it heard the bell, even though there was no food in sight.

Passing Messages On

Impulses pass from one nerve cell to another across tiny gaps called *synapses*. Some large nerve cells may be linked to as many as a thousand other nerve cells by synapses. The electrical impulse has to be changed into a chemical message, which "jumps across" the gap. The chemical message triggers an electrical impulse in the next nerve cell. There may be as many as a hundred different chemicals able to pass on messages in the central nervous system of a complex animal. The large number of chemicals helps to prevent communications from getting confused.

Nerve impulses are all the same but the number of impulses that travel along the nerves can vary and may reach up to a thousand impulses a second. The way the brain acts on information from the nerve impulses depends on where they have come from. Nerves carrying impulses from receptor cells in the skin to the spinal cord or the brain are called *sensory nerves*. Nerves carrying impulses out from the brain or spinal cord to the rest of the body are called *motor nerves*. These nerves cause muscles to move.

Cell body of nerve cell

Dendrites

Nucleus

In the circle below is an enlarged view of the gap between one nerve cell and the next. This is called a *synapse*. Chemicals released from one nerve cell cross the synapse and trigger an electrical impulse in the next nerve cell.

End of axon

Synapse

Myelin sheath round axon

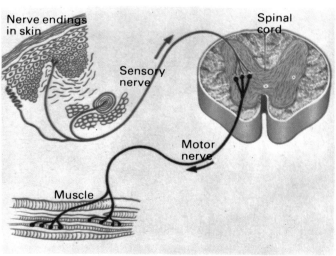

Nerve endings in skin

Sensory nerve

Spinal cord

Motor nerve

Muscle

Above: The pathway followed by nerve impulses in a reflex action. This is an automatic response that does not involve the brain. Impulses travel to the spinal cord along sensory nerves and back out to muscles along motor nerves.
Below and left: Diagram to show how human nerve cells link together to carry nerve impulses. The impulses are passed from one nerve cell to another across tiny gaps called *synapses*.

Dendrites   Nerve fibre

Branching end of motor neurone in muscles

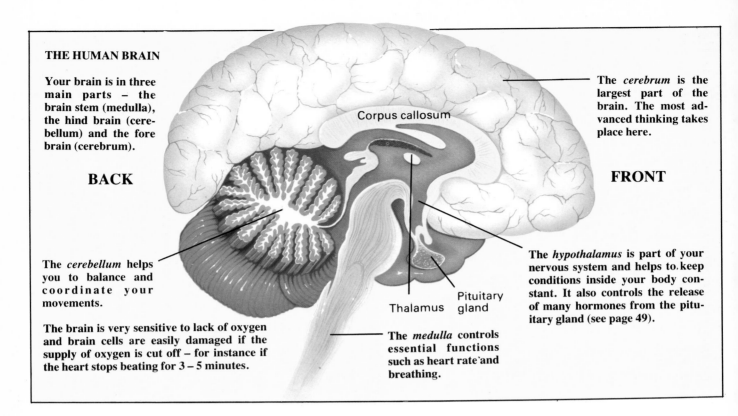

THE HUMAN BRAIN

Your brain is in three main parts – the brain stem (medulla), the hind brain (cerebellum) and the fore brain (cerebrum).

BACK

The *cerebrum* is the largest part of the brain. The most advanced thinking takes place here.

Corpus callosum

FRONT

The *cerebellum* helps you to balance and coordinate your movements.

The brain is very sensitive to lack of oxygen and brain cells are easily damaged if the supply of oxygen is cut off – for instance if the heart stops beating for 3 – 5 minutes.

The *hypothalamus* is part of your nervous system and helps to keep conditions inside your body constant. It also controls the release of many hormones from the pituitary gland (see page 49).

Thalamus

Pituitary gland

The *medulla* controls essential functions such as heart rate and breathing.

The Control Center

A brain is rather like a computer. It takes in information, processes it and sends out the results of its processing as instructions to control and coordinate all the other organs in your body. Your brain contains about 10,000 million nerve cells and is far more complex and versatile than any computer. No computer can do anything until it has been programmed by a human brain. People use up to twenty percent of their total energy to supply enough fuel for their massive brain.

The brain of any animal has to keep body processes running automatically and at the same time respond to the environment, which may be constantly changing.

Animal brains receive an uninterrupted flow of signals from their sensory nerves. This information is continuously coordinated and signals go out to all parts of the body. As a general rule, large animals have large brains. They need large brains to control their big bodies. And the development of an animal's brain reflects its needs and way of life. For example, a dog has a large area of its brain to deal with smells. A dolphin's brain is well developed to process the sounds it relies on to navigate underwater.

The Two Halves of the Brain

The large, folded part of your brain, the *cerebrum*, is in two halves, which are called the left and right hemispheres. The nerves cross over as they enter your brain so that the left hemisphere controls the right side of your body and the right hemisphere controls the left side. Each hemisphere has specialized areas. Most people depend more on the left hemisphere of their brain than the right. This is why most people are right-handed.

In right-handed people, the left hemisphere is responsible for speech, reading, writing and logical thinking. The right hemisphere is more important in appreciating music, artistic ability, creativity and the emotions. Scientists have been able to plot the areas of the brain responsible for many functions and feelings by applying an electrode to the exposed brain during operations. It is surprising that the brain, which has by far the most nerve cells of any organ in the body, cannot sense pain.

Very little is known about some areas of the brain, such as those that control memory. Memory can probably be improved by regular use, as the connections between the nerve cells become like well-worn paths in your brain.

Smell, Taste and Touch

Receptor cells at the back of your nose are sensitive to chemicals dissolved in the mucus of your nose. Impulses then travel to certain areas of the brain, giving us sensations of smell. Human beings can distinguish about 3,000 different smells.

Taste works in a similar way. The sensory cells (*taste buds*) are in your tongue. A combination of our senses of taste and smell helps us to taste food.

In people and many other animals all parts of the skin are sensitive to touch. Different kinds of receptors in the skin each respond mainly to a particular stimulus, such as heat, cold or pain.

Right below: The position of the main endocrine glands in the human body and some of the main hormones they produce. The testes and ovaries are included for simplicity although they do not occur in the same body.

NERVES OF THE SKIN

Pressure sensitive endings

Cold receptors

Heat receptors

Nerve fibers round base of hair

Touch receptors

Nerve endings sensitive to pain

Some of the different sensory receptors in the skin, which each respond mainly to a particular stimulus, such as heat, cold, pain or touch. The numbers of these receptors vary over the body surface. For example, the fingertips have many touch receptors.

Chemical Messengers

Along with a nervous system, many animals have a second control system based on chemical substances called *hormones*. In humans, they are produced mainly by special glands, called *endocrine glands*, and poured directly into the bloodstream. They reach their targets as blood flows through the body.

Hormones control major processes in the body including growth, water balance, reproduction and your reaction to an emergency. All hormones are broken down when they reach the liver. Hormones cannot control body processes efficiently unless they are maintained at the right level in the blood. This level is controlled by the hypothalamus and pituitary gland, using a balancing system called *feedback*.

Right above: The hypothalamus and the pituitary gland control hormone levels in the blood by a balancing system known as *feedback*. For example, the pituitary controls the amount of thyroxine in the blood by producing a thyroid-stimulating hormone (TSH). The pituitary detects high or low levels of thyroxine in the blood and releases less or more TSH to keep the level constant. But sometimes the body's needs for thyroxine rise above or fall below the constant level. (More thyroxine is needed to increase heat production in cold weather for instance.) This information is fed through the hypothalamus (part of the brain). The hypothalamus controls the amount of TSH produced by the pituitary by producing a substance called a releasing factor (RF). You can see how this works if you follow the arrows.

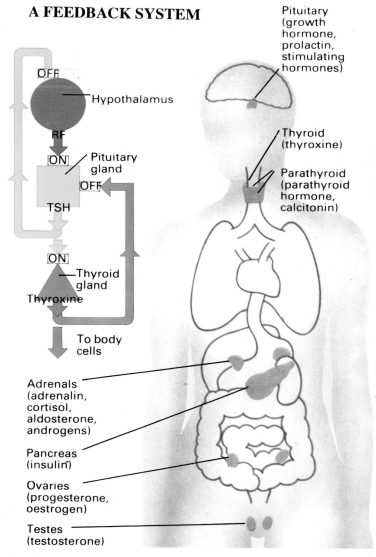

A FEEDBACK SYSTEM

OFF — Hypothalamus

RF

ON / Pituitary gland

OFF

TSH

ON — Thyroid gland

Thyroxine

To body cells

Pituitary (growth hormone, prolactin, stimulating hormones)

Thyroid (thyroxine)

Parathyroid (parathyroid hormone, calcitonin)

Adrenals (adrenalin, cortisol, aldosterone, androgens)

Pancreas (insulin)

Ovaries (progesterone, oestrogen)

Testes (testosterone)

49

Seeing the World

Eyes provide a way for nerve endings to be stimulated by light waves. And in this way, the human eye and the eyes of all but the simplest of animals can gather a vast amount of information about the outside world.

The Human Eye

The human eye is often compared to a camera. Both have lenses to bring objects into focus on a light sensitive area. Both have openings that control the amount of light entering. The eye, however, is more complicated than any camera.

The human eye is enclosed by three layers. We can see part of the outer layer, the *sclera*, as the white of the eye. It is formed of tough material and protects the eye. The middle layer, the *choroid*, is made of tissues with many blood vessels to nourish the eye. The inner layer, the *retina*, is formed of nerve endings from the optic nerve, which have spread out to line the inside of the eye.

The colored part of your eye is called the *iris*.

It gets its color from pigments it contains. Blue eyes, however, have no pigment. Babies often start life with blue eyes, which change color when they start producing pigment. The *pupil* is the hole through the colored iris. Around the pupil is a sphincter muscle. When it contracts, your pupil gets smaller. Other muscles, called radial muscles, reach from the pupil to the outer rim of the iris. When they contract, they pull the iris back and the pupil becomes larger. This lets more light into the eye.

The *lens* focuses light waves onto the light-sensitive cells of the retina – you can see how this works in the diagram below. Light stimulates the cells of the retina to send impulses through the optic nerve to the brain. And it is in the brain that "seeing" really takes place. The vast complexity of the brain translates nerve impulses into our view of the world around us. For instance, the image of everything we see is focused upside down on the retina but the brain turns the images right side up.

THE HUMAN EYE

In the diagram to the left you can see inside the human eye. The light waves entering the eye are bent (refracted) by the lens so they meet on the back of the eye, which is called the *retina*. (The image is upside down because the rays of light cross over behind the lens.) The retina contains millions of sensory cells, which are switched on by the light and send nerve impulses to the brain. The brain interprets the impulses so that you can see.

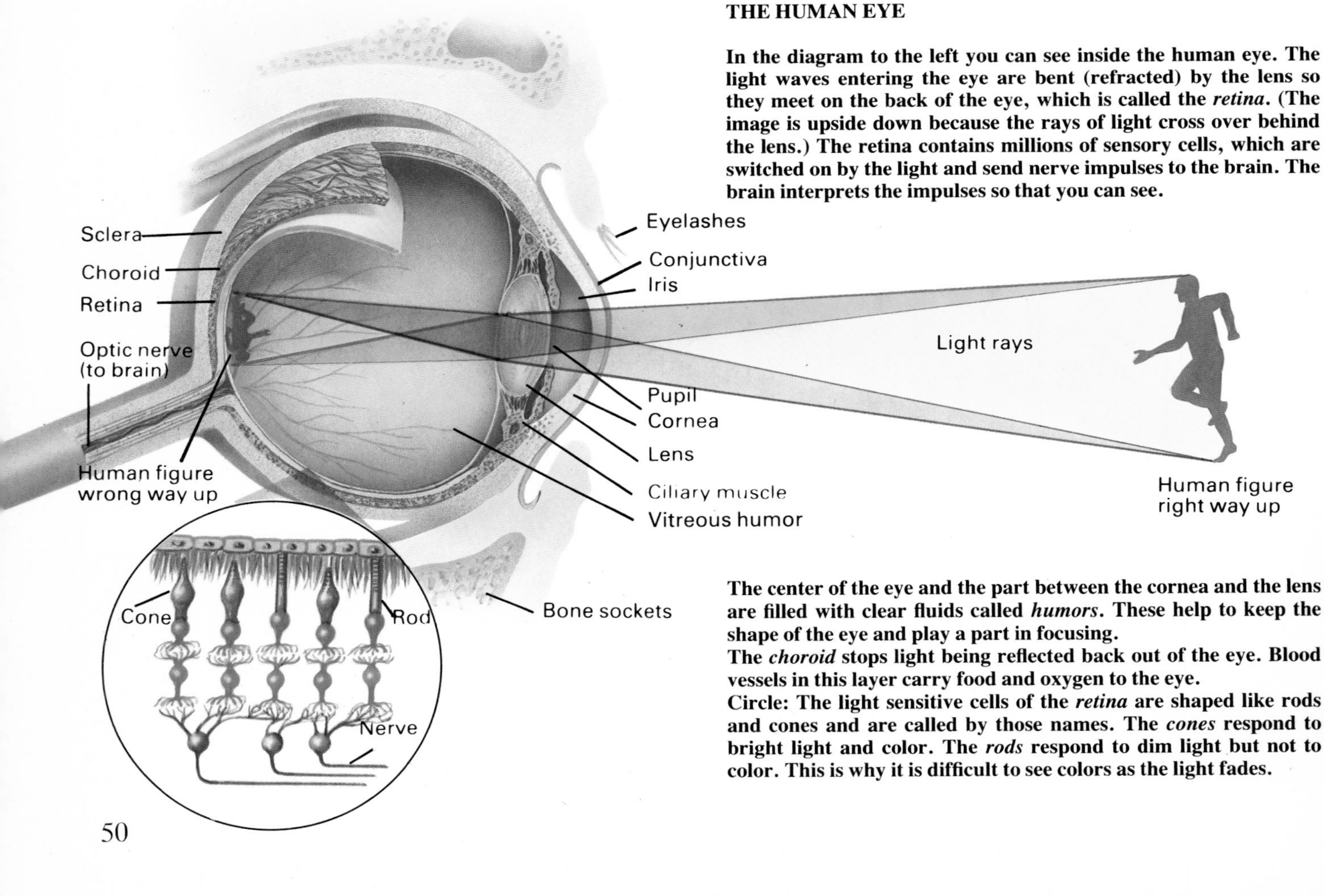

Sclera
Choroid
Retina
Optic nerve (to brain)
Human figure wrong way up
Cone
Rod
Nerve
Bone sockets
Eyelashes
Conjunctiva
Iris
Light rays
Pupil
Cornea
Lens
Ciliary muscle
Vitreous humor
Human figure right way up

The center of the eye and the part between the cornea and the lens are filled with clear fluids called *humors*. These help to keep the shape of the eye and play a part in focusing.

The *choroid* stops light being reflected back out of the eye. Blood vessels in this layer carry food and oxygen to the eye.

Circle: The light sensitive cells of the *retina* are shaped like rods and cones and are called by those names. The *cones* respond to bright light and color. The *rods* respond to dim light but not to color. This is why it is difficult to see colors as the light fades.

How the Lens Works

If your vision is perfect, you can focus on anything from infinity to book-reading distance. Focusing is carried out by the lens, which bends (refracts) the light rays so they meet on the retina at the back of the eye.

Light from a nearby object has to be bent more than light from a distant object. This is possible because the lens is pliable and muscles pull it into a different shape. If you are looking at a nearby object, the muscles relax, which makes the lens rounder. If you are looking at a distant object, the muscles contract, which makes the lens flatter.

Failure of the eyes to focus is a common fault, especially as we grow older. This can usually be corrected by wearing glasses, which make sure the light rays are bent at the right angle when they enter the eye. As long as this happens, they will meet exactly on the back of the retina and we can see clearly. Only one other group of animals, the squid and octopuses, have eyes similar to those of humans and other vertebrates.

FARSIGHTEDNESS

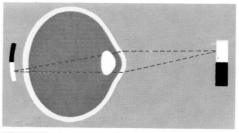

Farsighted people can focus on things a long way off but not close up. The rays focus behind the retina.

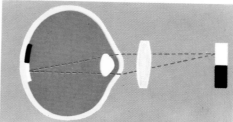

Farsightedness can be corrected by wearing lenses that make the light rays bend inward (converge) before they enter the eyes.

NEARSIGHTEDNESS

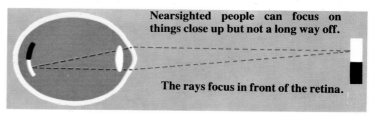

Nearsighted people can focus on things close up but not a long way off.

The rays focus in front of the retina.

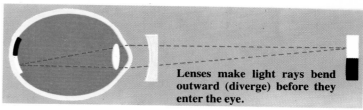

Lenses make light rays bend outward (diverge) before they enter the eye.

Below left: Owls, like most birds of prey, have their eyes at the front of the head. This helps them to see ahead very clearly and find prey more easily. They have to turn their heads to keep track of objects and can almost turn them in a full circle.

Above: Most birds have eyes at the side of the head so they can watch for danger without turning the head.

Right: Look carefully at this picture. Do you see a vase or two people facing each other? Your brain sees the picture in both ways and cannot choose between them.

Below: The cube on the left looks larger because the brain uses clues from the background to work out the size and position of objects. It is fooled by the background lines.

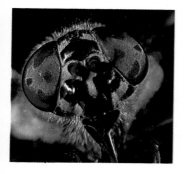

Left: The head of a horsefly showing the large compound eyes which are made up of many tiny eyes called *ommatidia*. Each ommatidium forms a picture of the world immediately in front of it. Insects have very large eyes and are good at detecting movement.

Are all these cubes the same size?

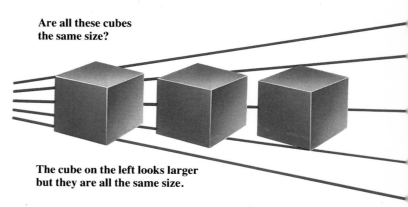

The cube on the left looks larger but they are all the same size.

51

Sound and Hearing

Sound waves are vibrations in the air. These vibrations are caught by the outer part of your ear – the only part you can see. The other two parts of your ear (the middle and inner ear) are hidden inside your head where they are protected by the bones of the skull. The outer ear funnels vibrations down the ear hole to your eardrum. This vibrates at the same rate as the sound waves hitting it and tiny bones on the other side of the eardrum pick up the vibrations. They carry them across to the inner ear where they trigger nerve impulses, which travel to the brain. The brain interprets the impulses as sound.

The ears of many other animals work on the same principle. Whales and dolphins have probably the most advanced hearing of all. Some of them, such as the killer whale, may "see" underwater by sound waves as well as we see by light waves.

Your Outer Ear

Sound waves collected by your outer ear pass down the ear canal. The hairs and wax along this canal trap dust and other particles so they do not damage the *eardrum*. The eardrum is a thin sheet of skin slightly over an inch (3 centimeters) inside the canal.

Your Middle Ear

Three tiny, delicate bones form a chain carrying sound vibrations across the cavity of the middle ear. Because of their shapes, these bones are called the *hammer*, *anvil* and the *stirrup*. The base of the stirrup covers the oval window, a thin sheet of skin at the entrance to the inner ear. The oval window vibrates when the stirrup vibrates.

Vibrations of the eardrum become more than twenty times greater within the middle ear. This is due to the structure of the three bones and the fact that the oval window is much smaller than the eardrum. The middle ear is connected to the throat by a narrow tube, 1.5 inches (four centimeters) long, which opens automatically when you swallow or yawn. This helps to keep the pressure equal inside and outside the eardrum.

Above: The head of a killer whale. Whales have very acute hearing and communicate with each other by making a variety of sounds. They also produce ultrasonic pulses which bounce back from objects in the water and on the seabed. This helps the whale to find food and navigate through the ocean depths.
Below: Frogs have well-developed and highly sensitive ears. They pick up sounds by means of a large ear drum – you can see this just behind the eye in this common frog.

Below: Fish have a line of sense organs called a *lateral line* down each side of the body. This detects changes in pressure, including vibrations (low frequency sounds) in the water.

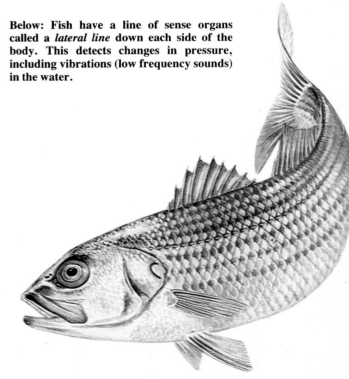

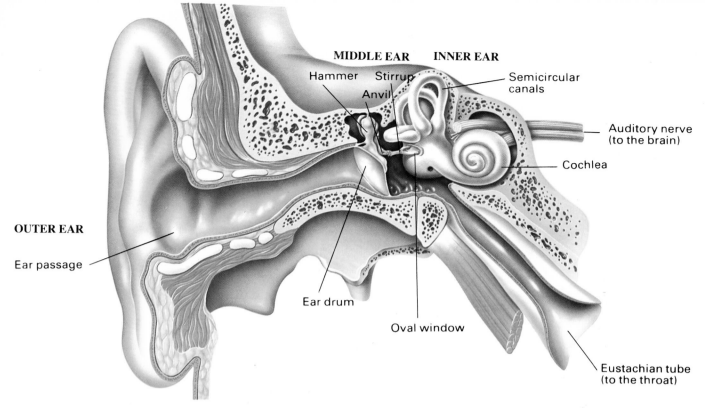

MIDDLE EAR　**INNER EAR**

Hammer　Stirrup

Anvil

Semicircular canals

Auditory nerve (to the brain)

Cochlea

OUTER EAR

Ear passage

Ear drum

Oval window

Eustachian tube (to the throat)

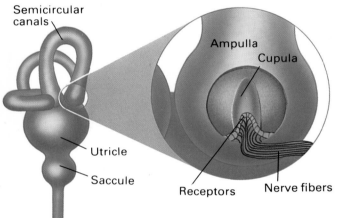

Semicircular canals

Ampulla

Cupula

Utricle

Saccule

Receptors　Nerve fibers

Above: The organ in the inner ear that helps you to balance. Each semicircular canal contains a swollen area called the *ampulla*. This contains receptor cells. As you tilt your head, fluid presses on the sensory hairs of the receptor cells and triggers electrical nerve impulses. These are sent to the cerebellum of your brain. When you spin around and around and then stop, the fluid in your semicircular canals continues to swirl for a while as though you were still moving. This confuses your brain and makes you feel dizzy.

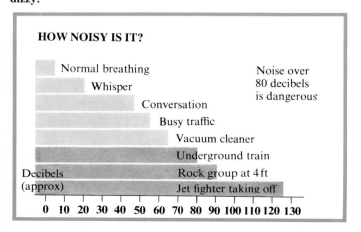

HOW NOISY IS IT?

Normal breathing

Whisper

Noise over 80 decibels is dangerous

Conversation

Busy traffic

Vacuum cleaner

Underground train

Decibels (approx)

Rock group at 4 ft

Jet fighter taking off

0 10 20 30 40 50 60 70 80 90 100 110 120 130

Above: A section through the human ear showing the three main parts. The *outer ear* collects sounds from the air and the *middle ear* carries the vibrations across to the inner ear. In the *inner ear*, the vibrations trigger off nerve impulses, which travel to the brain.

Your Inner Ear

The inner ear is deep within the skull, behind and slightly below your eyeball. It is full of fluid and contains two elaborate structures, one for hearing (the *cochlea*) and the other for balance.

Sound vibrations from the oval window travel through the fluid-filled tube called the cochlea, which is coiled like the shell of a snail. They cause the movement of tiny, hair-like nerve endings – about 25,000 in each ear. Receptor cells convert the movements to electrical signals (nerve impulses), which travel to the brain. The brain interprets these impulses as sounds. Bigger vibrations cause the sensory cells to send more impulses to the brain and we hear louder sounds. With two ears, animals can tell where a sound is coming from because one ear will usually receive a stronger signal than the other.

The other structure of the inner ear helps you to keep your balance. It consists of three semicircular canals and two tiny sacs, called the *utricle* and the *saccule*. The whole structure is filled with fluid called *endolymph*. The sacs tell you what position your head is in and the canals tell you what direction it is moving in.

53

Skin, Fur, and Feathers

Skin protects an animal's body from the outside world and provides a barrier against infection. It is a waterproof covering, which prevents animals from drying out. In mammals and birds, it helps to maintain a constant body temperature. The skin also has vast numbers of sensory cells and nerve endings within it so it is sensitive to touch, pressure, pain and temperature. In some mammals, such as the porcupine, the hairs in the skin are thickened up into sharp spines, which help to protect the animal from attack. And in animals like the rhinoceros, the horns are made of lots of hairs fused together.

Your Skin

Your skin is made of two main layers – the top part is called the *epidermis* and the thick layer underneath is called the *dermis*. The epidermis consists of three layers of cells arranged like the bricks in a wall. New cells are constantly being formed in the bottom layer, the *malpighian* layer. In the middle is the *granular* layer. The lower cells of this layer are living but they merge into an outer layer of dead cells, called the *cornified* layer. Cells are constantly being shed or worn away from this layer.

The cornified layer in humans can be many cells deep. But in invertebrates, such as insects, the whole epidermis is only one cell thick. This thin layer usually produces the insect's cuticle (its exoskeleton). The cuticle prevents water being lost and gives protection against injury. But it is only useful on a small body. The cuticle of an insect the size of a dog or a sheep would be too heavy for the animal's muscles to move.

Underneath your epidermis lies the dermis. It is made of connective tissues and flexible collagen fibers. The dermis has many blood capillaries and sensory cells as well as sweat glands and *hair follicles*.

A hair follicle is a deep, narrow hole in the skin. Cells grow continuously at the base of the follicle and push the older cells up the follicle. As they do so, they absorb *keratin* (a tough fibrous protein) and die. This forms the hair. *Sebaceous glands* open into the follicle, providing oil for hair and skin. Below the dermis lies *adipose tissue* in which fat is stored.

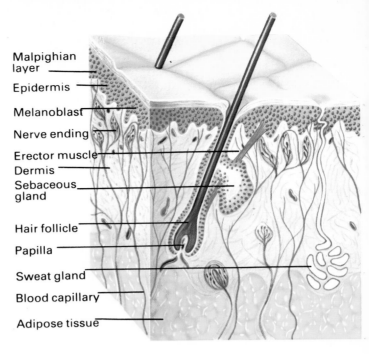

Diagram showing the main structures in human skin. Your skin is the largest organ in your body. The skin of an average adult weighs 8 to 10 pounds (3.5 to 4.5 kilograms) and covers an area of about 22 square feet (2 square meters).

Warming Up and Cooling Down

The most complex job of your skin is temperature control. The brain keeps a constant check on the temperature of the blood. If it goes above or below 98.6 degrees fahrenheit (36.8 degrees celsius), the brain sends nerve signals to the arteries feeding blood to the capillaries of the skin. These arteries open wider so that more blood reaches the surface of the skin, which may become reddish. Heat can then escape from the skin surface.

When the body gets too cold, the same capillaries narrow, which cuts down the amount of blood reaching the skin surface and keeps heat in the body.

The blood vessels, sweat glands and hairs in your skin all work together to warm you up or cool you down so that your body temperature stays roughly the same.

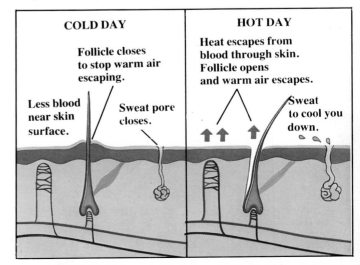

Fur and feathers help mammals and birds to maintain a constant body temperature. Minute muscle fibers are attached to the individual hair follicles. Mammals can therefore pull up their fur, which creates air spaces. This traps heat because air is a poor conductor of heat. Birds fluff up their feathers in the same way and this helps to keep them warm for the same reason.

We show signs of this reaction when we get goose pimples, which occur when tiny muscles attached to our hair follicles contract to make our body hairs stand on end. This response was probably inherited from our distant ancestors, who had plenty of hair. It is not much use to us today, so we rely more on the fatty tissues below the skin and clothes to keep us warm.

Shivering is another automatic response we have to cold. It moves our muscles, which "burns" food and releases energy to keep us warm.

The Role of Sweat Glands

Your skin also helps to get rid of waste products, such as urea and salts. It does this via *sweat glands* – there are two to three million of them in your skin. A sweat gland consists of a coiled tube leading to the surface of the skin. The tube gathers fluid from blood capillaries and surrounding cells and releases it from the skin surface. This also helps to cool you down.

Many other mammals have few sweat glands and birds have none. They have to lose heat in other ways. Birds do this by opening their beak, while dogs sit with their wet tongues hanging out on hot days. The sweat glands on a dog are mainly on the pads of the feet.

Above: Close-up of a pheasant's feather. Feathers are strong and tough but very light. The central shaft or quill of a feather is hollow. It has many *barbs* either side, which are linked by tiny hooks called *barbules*.

Shaft
Barbs
Barbules

Left: Close-up of the scales on a butterfly's wing. The scales are in fact flattened hairs and they provide the colors on the wings. Butterflies and moths belong to a group of insects called *Lepidoptera*, which means "scaly winged."

Below: No two people in the world have the same fingerprints. Even the fingerprints of identical twins are different. This is why fingerprints help the police to identify criminals.

Right: The amazing spiral horns of the markhor (a wild goat) measure as much as five feet in length. Horns are made of a tightly packed fiber called *keratin*.

New Generations

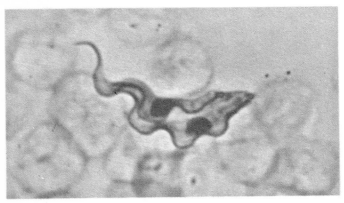

Hydra

Branch grows out.

Tentacles and mouth develop.

Ready to break away

Above: Hydra is a many-celled animal (a coelenterate) that lives in fresh water. It usually reproduces asexually by *budding*. A new hydra grows out from the side of the parent and eventually drops off to lead a separate life.

Below: A *trypanosome* dividing into two – look for the two nuclei. *Trypanosomes* are parasitic protozoa that cause diseases in people, horses and cattle.

Below: *Obelia* is an animal that lives in the sea in colonies attached to rocks. It develops two types of branches called *polyps*. The feeding polyps capture food with their tentacles. The reproductive polyps produce male and female *medusa*, which look like tiny jellyfish. These swim off into the water and, when they are mature, the male releases sperm and the female releases eggs. When a sperm fertilizes an egg, it develops into a swimming larva called a *planula*. This settles onto a rock and grows into a new obelia colony.

Animals have to produce new individuals like themselves for their species to survive. There are two kinds of reproduction, *sexual* and *asexual* ("a" means *without*). Most animals reproduce sexually but some, particularly the simplest animals, reproduce asexually as well.

Asexual reproduction involves only one parent and produces new individuals which are exact copies of that parent. No sex cells are involved. Although it is a rapid method of reproduction, the animals do not change from one generation to the next so they cannot adapt to changes in their surroundings. Two of the most common methods of asexual reproduction are when one single-celled animal divides into two and when a new individual grows out from its parent in a process called *budding*.

Sexual reproduction involves two parents and produces new individuals which are different from their parents. This allows animals to change from one generation to another so they are more likely to survive if conditions around them change.

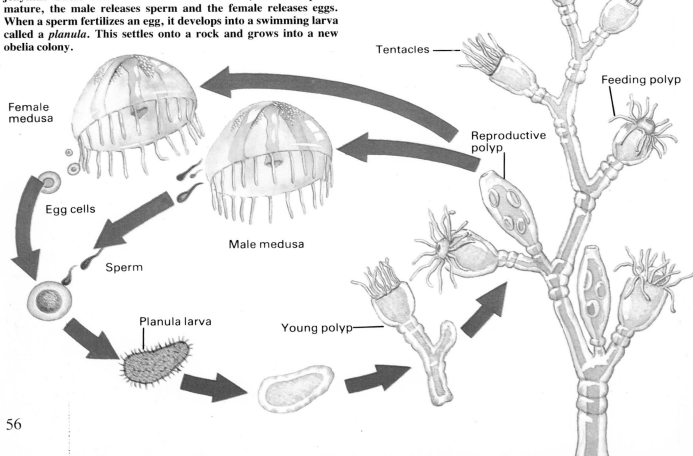

Female medusa

Egg cells

Sperm

Male medusa

Planula larva

Young polyp

Tentacles

Feeding polyp

Reproductive polyp

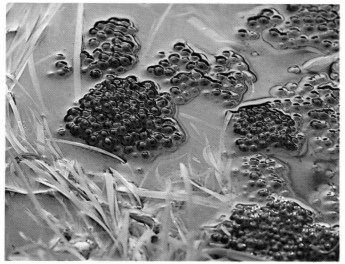

Frog
spawn

Tadpole – about
6 weeks old

Adult
Common frog

Left: Recently laid frog spawn floating on the surface of a pond. Above: The female common frog lays her jelly-covered eggs (spawn) in the spring. As they emerge into the water, the male releases his sperm onto them. The sperm swim through the jelly and fertilize the eggs. The tadpoles hatch after about 10 days. They take about three to four months to develop into young frogs.

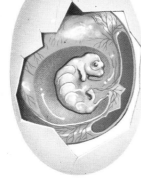

Left: The tough, leathery shell of a reptile's egg keeps moisture in and helps to stop the egg drying out. The double layer of membranes shields the embryo from external shocks and changes in temperature. A third membrane, the allantois, collects wastes excreted by the embryo. Food is provided by a yolk sac and fed to the embryo through blood vessels.

THE LIFE CYCLE OF A BUTTERFLY

This swallowtail butterfly starts life as an egg. It hatches into a caterpillar, which feeds on leaves. It changes its skin several times as it grows. Then it attaches itself to a leaf or twig and turns into a pupa. Inside this protective coating, it changes into a butterfly. Finally, the pupa splits open and an adult butterfly pushes its way out. The butterfly pumps blood into its wings to make them unfold and waits for its wings to dry before flying away.

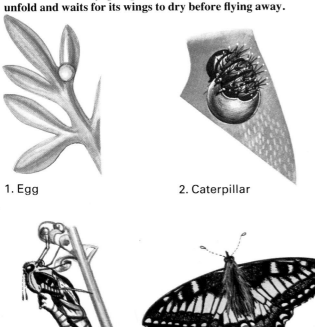

1. Egg

2. Caterpillar

3. Pupa

4. Adult

In sexual reproduction, two sex cells have to fuse together. One of these cells comes from a female animal and is called an egg cell or *ovum* (plural *ova*). The other sex cell comes from a male animal and is called a *sperm cell*. The sex cells are known as *gametes* and the fusing of two gametes is called *fertilization*. The result of fertilization is a cell called a *zygote*, from which a new individual can develop. The zygote contains a mixture of the genetic instructions from two individuals in the DNA molecules in its nucleus. (You can find out more about genetic instructions later in the book.) They control the characteristics of an animal, including its appearance and the chemical processes that go on inside its body.

In some animals, including fish and amphibians such as frogs, fertilization takes place outside the body. The female lays her eggs and the male fertilizes them by placing sperm on them afterward. In birds, the eggs are fertilized inside the body of the female. The male passes sperm into the egg tubes and fertilizes the eggs before they are laid. The chick does not develop much before the egg is laid, however.

The eggs are also fertilized inside the female's body in mammals and the young develop there as well. Some, such as kangaroos, are born in a very immature state but others, such as zebras, are able to run about soon after they are born. All mammals feed their young with milk produced in glands on the mother's body. They look after their young following birth more than any other animals do.

57

New Human Life

Human beings reproduce sexually. It takes just one sperm cell to combine with one ovum in a woman's body to produce a new cell, which grows and develops into a baby in the woman's womb (*uterus*).

The male and female reproductive systems start working fully at *puberty*. This is about 11 years in females and 13 in males but the age varies a lot between individuals.

As both sexes develop, they grow pubic hair and hair under the arms. In females, the breasts develop, the hips widen, the reproductive organs grow and develop and the *menstrual cycle* (monthly periods) begins. In males, the beard starts to grow, the larynx (Adam's apple) enlarges and the voice deepens, the shoulders and chest broaden, the reproductive organs develop and sperm are produced. The body changes at puberty enable a mature ovum and sperm cell to come together and to prepare the female's body for a baby.

The Male Reproductive System

The main organs of the male reproductive system are the testes, which produce sperm, and the penis, which releases the sperm.

The testes hang outside the body in a loose bag of skin called the *scrotum*. This helps to keep them cool. The temperature inside the body is too warm for sperm production to be very efficient. Inside each testicle are up to a thousand tiny coiled tubes where sperm are produced. They are stored in a long, coiled tube called the *epididymis*, which is about 20 feet (6 meters) long. It lies alongside each testicle.

During sexual excitement, the mature sperm move from the epididymis into the urethra, which is the outlet tube for the bladder. Along the way, fluids from the prostate gland are added to the sperm. Another gland (Cowper's gland) sterilizes the urethra for the passage of the sperm. The fluids protect the sperm from bacteria and provide nutrients. The mixture of fluids and sperm is called *semen*. The semen is discharged (ejaculated) into the woman's vagina during sexual intercourse. At this time the penis becomes larger and stiff (erect) because a lot of blood flows into it. One ejaculation contains hundreds of millions of sperm.

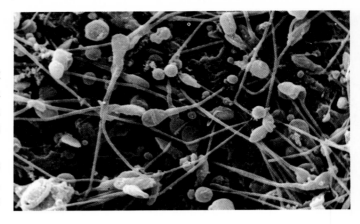

Above: Human sperm cells as they appear under a high-power electron microscope. Sperm are among the smallest cells in the body. The oval head contains 23 chromosomes, which may combine with the 23 chromosomes in a female ovum to form a fertilized egg cell. The tail of the sperm cell swings from side to side to push it along. The energy for this movement is stored in the thickest part of the tail.

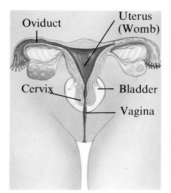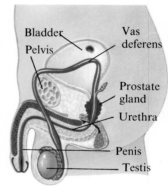

Above left: The human female reproductive system (from the front).
Above right: The human male reproductive system (from the side).
Below: A diagram showing the main stages in the human *menstrual cycle* (monthly period). The number of days given for each stage are only approximate as the timing of the cycle varies slightly from woman to woman. At the start of the cycle the lining of the uterus is shed, which causes bleeding (the period). A new lining then builds up. Sometime between days 10-18, an egg is released into one of the fallopian tubes (ovulation) and begins its journey toward the uterus. The lining of the uterus thickens, ready to receive a fertilized egg. If the egg is not fertilized, the lining is shed and a new cycle begins.

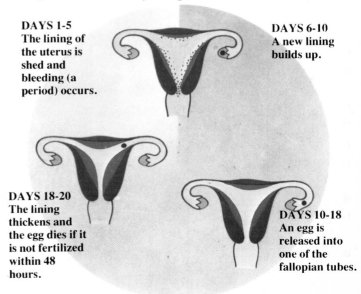

DAYS 1-5
The lining of the uterus is shed and bleeding (a period) occurs.

DAYS 6-10
A new lining builds up.

DAYS 18-20
The lining thickens and the egg dies if it is not fertilized within 48 hours.

DAYS 10-18
An egg is released into one of the fallopian tubes.

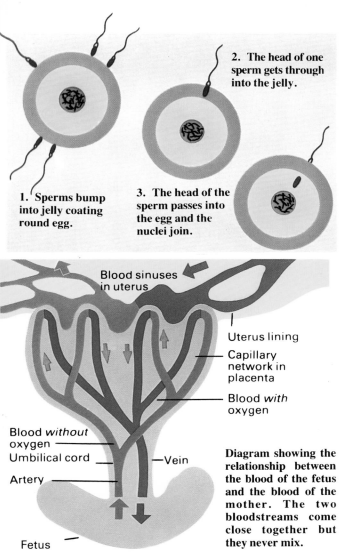

2. The head of one sperm gets through into the jelly.

1. Sperms bump into jelly coating round egg.

3. The head of the sperm passes into the egg and the nuclei join.

Blood sinuses in uterus

Uterus lining

Capillary network in placenta

Blood *with* oxygen

Blood *without* oxygen

Umbilical cord

Artery

Vein

Fetus

Diagram showing the relationship between the blood of the fetus and the blood of the mother. The two bloodstreams come close together but they never mix.

Left: Diagram showing the process of fertilization, which takes place in a fallopian tube. The sperm cells are attracted to the ovum by chemicals it produces. The head of one sperm cell manages to pass through the membrane of the ovum. Changes in the membrane prevent any other sperm cells from entering. The nucleus of the sperm cell fuses with the nucleus of the ovum to form a fertilized egg cell.

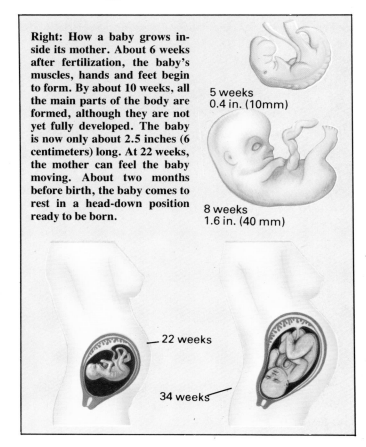

Right: How a baby grows inside its mother. About 6 weeks after fertilization, the baby's muscles, hands and feet begin to form. By about 10 weeks, all the main parts of the body are formed, although they are not yet fully developed. The baby is now only about 2.5 inches (6 centimeters) long. At 22 weeks, the mother can feel the baby moving. About two months before birth, the baby comes to rest in a head-down position ready to be born.

5 weeks
0.4 in. (10mm)

8 weeks
1.6 in. (40 mm)

22 weeks

34 weeks

The Female Reproductive System

The main organs of the female reproductive system are the two ovaries and the uterus. Thousands of immature eggs (ova) are stored in the ovaries from birth. Every month from puberty to the age of about 45, an ovum matures in one of the ovaries and is released. This is called *ovulation* and the time ovulation stops is called the *menopause*. The ovum is drawn down a tube called the *fallopian tube* (*oviduct*) to the uterus. On the way it may be fertilized by one of the sperm that swim up to the fallopian tubes after sexual intercourse.

Every month, from puberty to menopause, the lining of the uterus thickens to prepare for the arrival of a fertilized ovum. If the ovum is not fertilized, it is pushed out of the body, together with the inner part of the uterus lining and some blood, in the monthly period. The muscular contractions of the uterus walls sometimes cause pain and cramps at this time.

If the ovum is fertilized, it sinks into the uterus lining and in about two weeks a special organ called the *placenta* has formed. This is a barrier separating the mother's blood from the blood of the developing baby (the *embryo*). It allows food and oxygen to pass from the mother's blood to the blood of the embryo and wastes from the embryo to pass in the opposite direction. The baby is attached to the placenta by the *umbilical cord*.

During its growth, the baby lives in a fluid-filled bag called the *amniotic sac*, which helps to protect it from injury. A few weeks before the baby is born, it is positioned head-down over a ring of muscle called the *cervix*, the exit from the uterus. The time from fertilization to birth is usually about nine months.

At birth, the muscles of the uterus contract to push the baby out. The cervix, which is usually only about the size of a pinhole, enlarges to let the baby through. The amniotic sac breaks, releasing a gush of fluid down the vagina. More muscular contractions push the baby down the vagina into the outside world.

How a Baby Develop

A newborn baby can carry out some simple actions, such as gripping objects and sucking its mother's breast. At first it spends a lot of time asleep, except when it is hungry. After about a month, it can hold up its head if it is supported and after about six weeks, it can turn its head and smile. After about seven or eight weeks, it can roll over and reach for things.

A baby explores its surroundings to discover more about its world. Before it can crawl, it will touch its mother's face and any other objects it can reach. It will even put things in its mouth to get the feel of them. Gradually it learns to eat mashed up food, crawl and eventually toddle. All the time its understanding grows as it experiences new events and situations and learns from them.

There are many different ways of learning. One is by trial and error and another is by imitating (copying) other people. Babies begin to imitate when they are a few months old. By the time they are two years old, they are beginning to think. An important step in this process is the use of symbols and signs (such as drawings and words) to represent things they cannot see in front of them.

The development of thinking takes a long time but gradually children come to understand ideas such as number, length and weight, and by the time they reach adolescence they are able to reason and work out problems in a logical way.

Above: Babies have to learn to recognize things. At first, their mother's eyes interest them more than the rest of her head. But by the time the baby is three months old, it has learned to recognize the rest of its mother's face. Later still, a small child learns to recognize every feature of her face.
Below: These children are playing house. They have used toys and everyday objects to represent many different things. Play helps children to develop their imagination. It also gives them a chance to escape into a fantasy world when they can't understand things, and play helps them to learn about themselves.

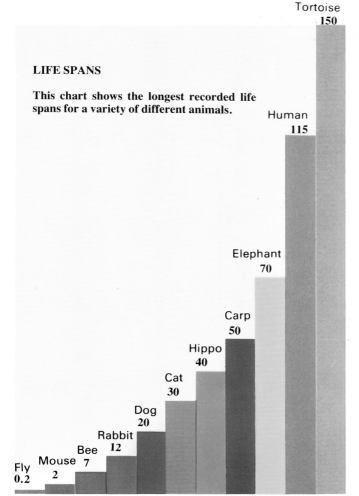

LIFE SPANS

This chart shows the longest recorded life spans for a variety of different animals.

Tortoise 150

Human 115

Elephant 70

Carp 50

Hippo 40

Cat 30

Dog 20

Rabbit 12

Bee 7

Mouse 2

Fly 0.2

Above: This photograph shows the contrast between the skin and muscles in an old person and in a young person.

How Long do they Live?

Scientists do not really understand why animals die. The cells in their bodies may just come to the end of their natural life, or there may be some kind of "body clock" which switches life off after a certain time.

In spite of the great advances in medical science, human beings today do not live much longer than those of past generations. Ages of 150 years are sometimes claimed, but in countries where reliable documents are available no one seems to live much beyond a hundred years. This still makes humans the longest-living mammals.

Reptiles, such as tortoises and turtles, do better. One tortoise lived at the barracks at Port Louis on the island of Mauritius for at least 150 years. It may be that these creatures escape aging to some extent because (unlike birds and mammals) they continue to grow throughout life. Plants also grow throughout life and some can live for several hundreds or even thousands of years. A bristlecone pine tree in the United

States is known to be 4,900 years old.

Many biologists believe that uncorrected errors in the chemical processes of life (such as faults in the production of *enzymes*) may be connected with aging. As the cells, tissues and organs deteriorate, they slowly age. Our *immune system*, which detects and destroys the faulty products of cells, becomes less efficient with age. Another factor is that the cells of our brain and nervous system die throughout life and cannot be replaced. A very old person has lost a considerable amount of brain cells.

One of the first research projects on aging was carried out by Dr. Clive McCay of Cornell University. He discovered that by underfeeding rats and mice he could lengthen their lives by about 50 percent. He showed that the right amount of food for the proper growth of rats and mice was not the same as the right amount of food for a long life. Studies have also shown that different parts of the human body age at different rates. But much work remains to be done.

Looking Inside Plants

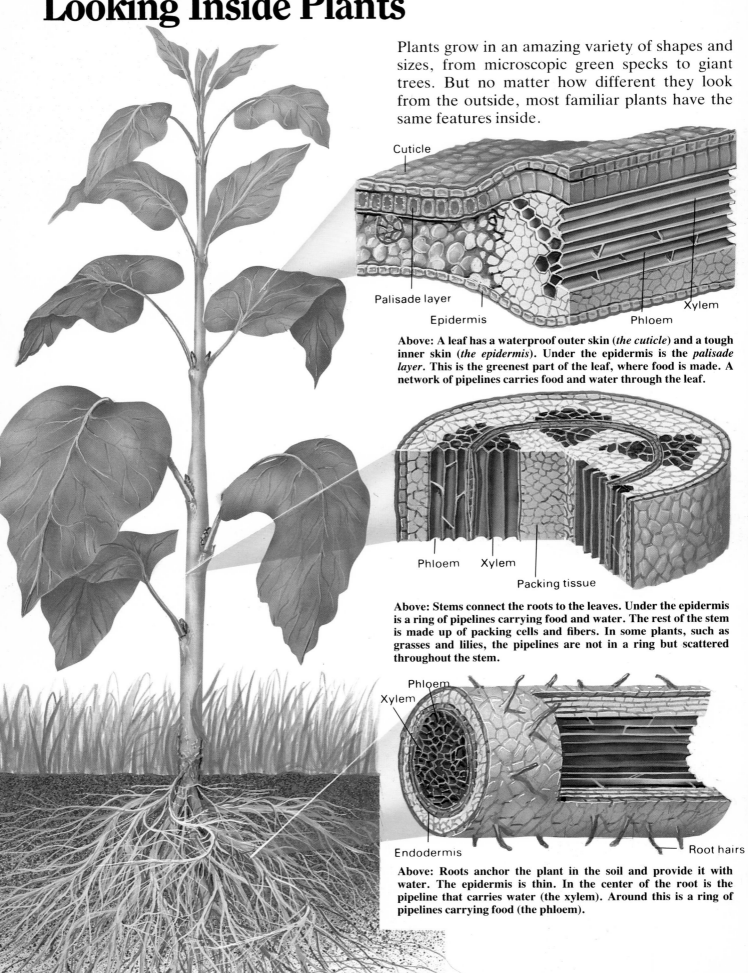

Plants grow in an amazing variety of shapes and sizes, from microscopic green specks to giant trees. But no matter how different they look from the outside, most familiar plants have the same features inside.

Cuticle

Palisade layer

Epidermis

Xylem

Phloem

Above: A leaf has a waterproof outer skin (*the cuticle*) and a tough inner skin (*the epidermis*). Under the epidermis is the *palisade layer*. This is the greenest part of the leaf, where food is made. A network of pipelines carries food and water through the leaf.

Phloem   Xylem

Packing tissue

Above: Stems connect the roots to the leaves. Under the epidermis is a ring of pipelines carrying food and water. The rest of the stem is made up of packing cells and fibers. In some plants, such as grasses and lilies, the pipelines are not in a ring but scattered throughout the stem.

Phloem

Xylem

Endodermis

Root hairs

Above: Roots anchor the plant in the soil and provide it with water. The epidermis is thin. In the center of the root is the pipeline that carries water (the xylem). Around this is a ring of pipelines carrying food (the phloem).

More About Leaves

You can usually recognize a plant from the shape of its leaves but sometimes a plant has more than one type of leaf. For example, the floating leaves of water crowfoot are rounded but the underwater leaves are feathery.

The branching pattern on the surface of a leaf is part of the network of pipelines that carry food and water around the plant. The pipelines are sometimes called *veins* and the main vein is called the *midrib*. The veins show up most clearly as the skeleton that remains on a dead leaf after the soft parts have been eaten away.

Some leaves have special features to help them survive in difficult climates. Furry leaves keep out the cold and thick fleshy leaves help to prevent the plant from drying out under a hot sun. Cactus spines and pine needles also help to prevent the plant from losing water. They are modified leaves. In tropical jungles, where it rains every day, some of the plants have leaves that end in long points (*drip tips*) so that the rain runs off. Some of the plants that live high up on the branches of the jungle trees have their leaves arranged in a cup shape to catch water. The leaves on a pineapple are arranged like this.

Plants also arrange their leaves so they get as much light as possible. You can see this for yourself if you look at a plant such as a begonia from above. Each leaf is placed so that it is not covered by another one and there are no gaps where you can see the soil below. Nobody knows exactly how plants do this.

Leaves are usually attached to stems by stalks. Where each stalk ends in one leaf, such as on a beech tree, the leaf is called a *simple leaf*. Where the leaf is divided so that each stalk looks as if it has several leaves (as on a horse chestnut tree) the leaf is known as a *compound leaf*. Some leaves have no stalks at all.

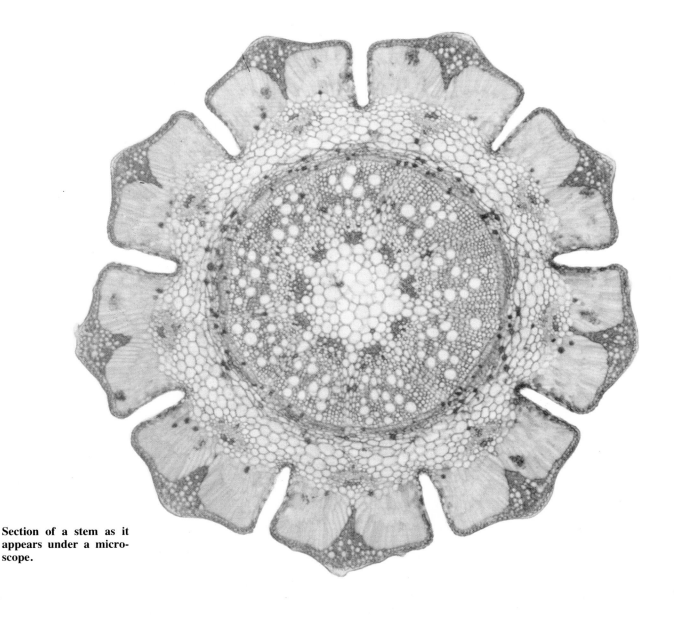

Section of a stem as it appears under a microscope.

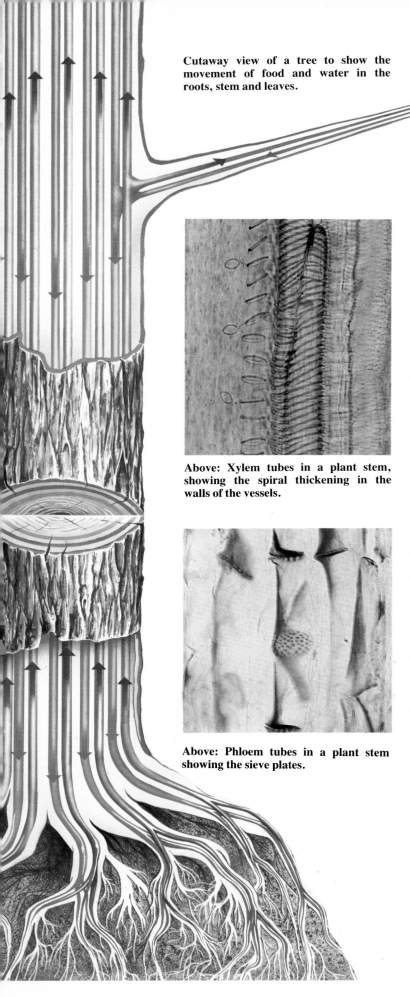

Cutaway view of a tree to show the movement of food and water in the roots, stem and leaves.

Above: Xylem tubes in a plant stem, showing the spiral thickening in the walls of the vessels.

Above: Phloem tubes in a plant stem showing the sieve plates.

Pipelines in Plants

Flowering plants have two kinds of pipelines in their leaves, stems and roots. One carries water and dissolved minerals. The other carries food.

Water Pipes

The pipelines that carry water are made up of rows of cells joined end to end with no walls between them. These cells are called *vessels* and they are dead structures. The vessels and the packing tissue around them are called *xylem*.

Water enters the plant through tiny fragile hairs just behind the tip of each root and travels across a few cells to join the main xylem in the middle of the root. From here it rises up the stem partly by being pushed from below and partly by being pulled from above. This flow of water is called the *transpiration stream* and the evaporation of water from the leaves is called *transpiration*.

Transpiration supplies all the water that plants need to make food and helps the cells to keep their shape, which stops the plant from wilting. Water evaporating from the leaves also helps to cool the plant down. Some trees lose their leaves in winter to cut down the amount of water they lose. It is often difficult for large trees to get enough water if the ground is frozen.

Food Pipes

Food is made in the leaves and travels around the plant in pipelines made of rows of living cells joined end to end. They are called *sieve tubes* because the end walls of the cells are full of holes. The sieve tubes and the packing tissue that supports them are called *phloem*. Food can travel up or down the stem in the phloem to reach any cells that need energy, such as those in growing regions. Sometimes food can travel up and down the plant at the same time but scientists are not sure how this is done.

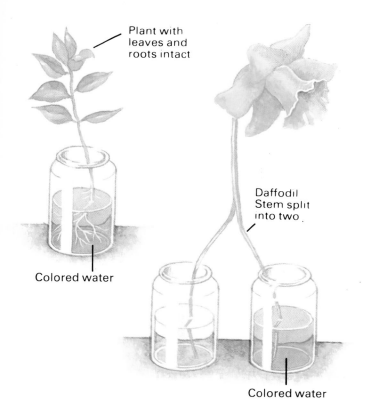

Plant with leaves and roots intact

Colored water

Daffodil Stem split into two

Colored water

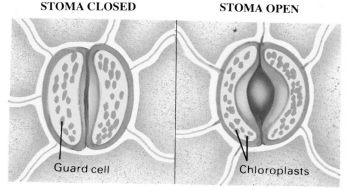

STOMA CLOSED   STOMA OPEN

Guard cell   Chloroplasts

Above: *Stomata* are tiny holes in the leaf that open and close to control the flow of gas and water vapor. The stoma opens as the guard cells bulge outward. When the stoma closes, the strong, elastic walls of the guard cells keep it tightly shut.

Left: Experiments to show how water is taken up by plants. Obtain a plant with its leaves and roots intact. Wash the soil off the roots and stand the plant in a jar of water containing a colored dye, such as ink, for 24 hours. Then cut the stem with a knife to see how far the dye has moved. If you use impatiens, which has a transparent stem, you will be able to see where the dye is. You could also try making colored flowers. Split the stem and put one half in water and the other in water containing a colored dye – as shown in the diagram to the left.

How Plants Breathe

All plants need to breathe, that is take in oxygen from the air and give out carbon dioxide. They use the oxygen to convert food into energy, which they use to drive their life processes. This is called *respiration* and it involves a series of chemical reactions inside the plant cells. Respiration takes place in animal cells as well but plants do not make breathing movements like animals. Gases simply pass in and out of the leaf or stem through tiny holes called *stomata*, which open and close to control the flow of gas. Woody stems have small raised pores called *lenticels* instead of stomata.

There is a network of air spaces between the cells of a leaf so that the gases do not have to travel far between the cells inside and the air outside. Before the gases can enter or leave a plant cell, they have to dissolve in the layer of moisture surrounding the cells.

Roots obtain the gases they need by absorbing oxygen that has dissolved in water in the soil. The cell walls are so thin that gases can get through them easily. Plants that live in water take in gases that have dissolved in the water that surrounds them.

How Stomata Work

If you look very carefully with a strong magnifying lens at the underside of a leaf, you may be able to see some circular shapes. Each one of these marks the site of a *stoma* (plural *stomata*), the tiny hole that automatically controls the flow of air and water vapor in and out of a leaf.

The opening of each stoma is surrounded by two sausage-shaped cells called *guard cells*. When there is a lot of water in the leaf, the guard cells absorb water and swell up. They bulge outward and separate, leaving a hole between them through which water vapor or gases can enter or leave. The stomata open when the plant is most active – usually when it is busy taking in and giving out gases while it is making food (see pages 66-67).

When the leaf loses water, the guard cells lose it too. As they shrink, the strong elastic walls between them pull the cells together and the stomata close.

There are more stomata on the underside of a leaf than on the upper surface. The upper surface is protected by a waterproof skin to prevent too much water being lost.

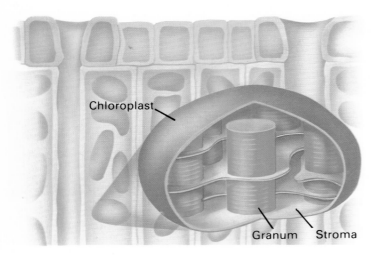
Chloroplast

Granum Stroma

Above: A view inside one of the chloroplasts in a leaf. Numerous sheet-like membranes called *lamellae* run from one end of the chloroplast to the other. In some areas, the lamellae are closer together and are arranged neatly on top of each other, rather like a stack of coins. Each group of lamellae is called a *granum* (plural *grana*). The grana hold chlorophyll molecules in the best possible position for trapping light energy from the sun. The grana and the rest of the lamellae are surrounded by a watery substance called the *stroma*. Light energy seems to be captured mainly in the grana, while carbohydrates are built up in the stroma.

Below: The diagrams below are a simplified summary of the chemical reactions during photosynthesis, the process by which plants make food.

Making Food With Light

Green plants are the only living things that can make their own food. They convert the sun's light energy into chemical energy, which they use to combine carbon dioxide and water to make sugar and oxygen. This process is called *photosynthesis*, which means "making things with light."

Plants make food mainly in their leaves, where a colored substance (a pigment) called *chlorophyll* traps the sun's energy. Chlorophyll is bright green and this is why so many plants are green. Plants that don't look green, such as many seaweeds, still contain chlorophyll but they also have other pigments, which mask the green color.

The recipe plants use to make food needs simple ingredients, just water and carbon dioxide. Land plants take in carbon dioxide from the air and water from the soil. Water travels up to the leaves in the xylem vessels and air enters

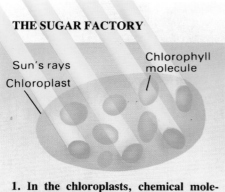

THE SUGAR FACTORY

Sun's rays
Chloroplast
Chlorophyll molecule

1. In the chloroplasts, chemical molecules called chlorophyll capture energy from sunlight.

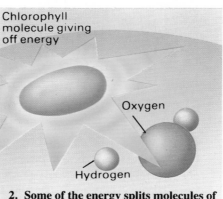

Chlorophyll molecule giving off energy

Oxygen

Hydrogen

2. Some of the energy splits molecules of water into hydrogen and oxygen.

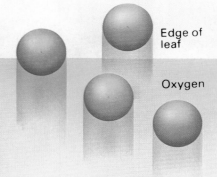

Edge of leaf

Oxygen

3. The oxygen is not needed and finds its way out of the leaf.

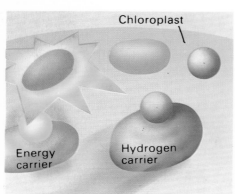

Chloroplast

Energy carrier

Hydrogen carrier

4. Back in the chloroplast, hydrogen and energy are picked up by special carrier molecules.

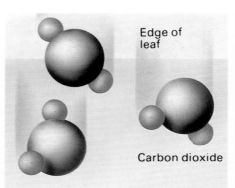

Edge of leaf

Carbon dioxide

5. Meanwhile, molecules of the gas carbon dioxide enter the leaf from the air.

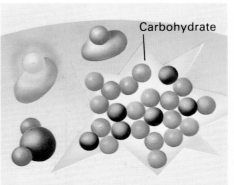

Carbohydrate

6. The energy joins the hydrogen and carbon dioxide to make sugar – food for the plant.

through tiny holes in the leaves and stems called stomata. (You can find out more about xylem and stomata on pages 64-65.) Water plants take in water and dissolved carbon dioxide all over their surfaces.

The basic food that plants make is a sort of sugar called a *carbohydrate*. It is rich in the energy trapped from sunlight. Some carbohydrates may be broken down by the plant immediately to release the energy needed for life processes. It is carried around the plant in the phloem tubes (see page 64) to all the cells that need energy. Some carbohydrates are stored for future use. Many plants store carbohydrates in special structures called *bulbs* and *tubers*. Potatoes are tubers and they are packed with starch.

Carbohydrates can also be converted into more complex substances such as the proteins in chlorophyll and enzymes. To make proteins, plants need extra chemical elements such as nitrogen, sulfur and phosphorus, which they take in as mineral salts.

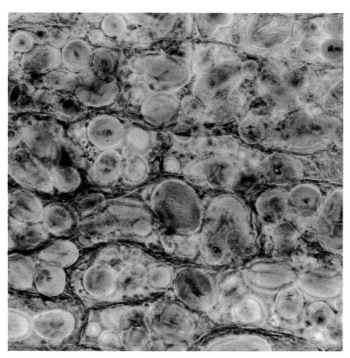

Some of the starch grains in a potato tuber, seen under a microscope. You can test for starch in a potato or plant leaf with a drop of iodine. You need to crush or boil the plant tissue first to break down the cell walls and allow the iodine to get inside the cells. Any starch will turn inky black.

Plants that Eat Animals

Some plants have an appetite for live animals, especially insects. The extra food probably helps them to survive in poor soils. Meat-eating plants trick their victims into deadly traps. They use digestive juices to turn the bodies of their prey into liquids they can absorb.

Robber Plants

Some plants have no chlorophyll and so cannot make their own food. They steal their food from other plants instead. They may eventually kill the plants they feed from. These plants are called *parasites* – you can find out more about parasites on page 89.

Left: Sundew plants trap insects in sticky red hairs that cover their leaves. The struggles of the insect make the hairs curl over it and stick it firmly to the leaf. It takes a day or two for a sundew to eat an insect.

Right: This ghostly orchid steals its food from trees with the help of a fungus. It soaks up food from the thread-like hyphae of a fungus that grow around the tree roots. The tangle of roots and hyphae in the soil give the orchid its name – bird's nest orchid.

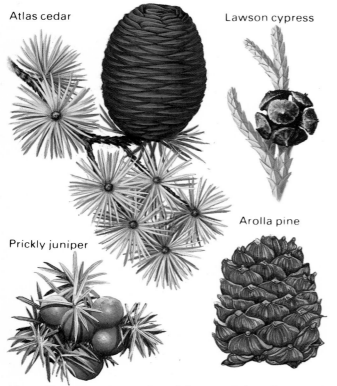

Cone scales are modified leaves.

Cross section through a female cone to show the seeds hidden beneath the woody scales. If you pick up a cone, you may be able to find some seeds flattened against the scales.

Atlas cedar

Lawson cypress

Arolla pine

Prickly juniper

Above: Cones come in a variety of shapes and sizes. Some, such as juniper, even look like berries. These are all female cones.
Below: Pollen grains from common juniper (left) and Scotch pine (right). Two air sacs on the Scotch pine pollen grain help it to drift on the wind.

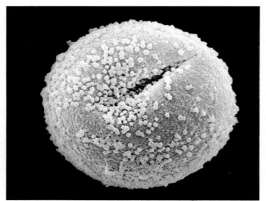

Pollen Packs — Cones and Flowers

Many new plants grow from seeds, which are produced in special structures called cones and flowers. Before a seed can develop, a male sex cell has to join with a female sex cell. These cells often come from different plants. Male sex cells are in the yellow dust called *pollen*, which is produced only by *gymnosperms* (plants with cones and their relatives) and *angiosperms* (plants with flowers). Female sex cells are called egg cells and they are inside a structure called an *ovule*, which is hidden inside a flower or cone.

In flowering plants the ovule is protected by the wall of a hollow structure called an *ovary*. But in gymnosperms, such as conifer trees, the ovule is naked and unprotected. Pollen travels from one flower or cone to another but the ovules stay where they are.

A Closer Look at Cones

Cones are always either male or female. A typical conifer, such as a cedar tree, produces female cones at the tips of the branches and male cones further down the shoot.

Female cones are small and soft to begin with and may take two or three years to develop into cones with woody scales. Tucked inside the scales, the naked ovules develop into seeds if they receive pollen from a male cone. When the seeds are fully grown, the scales open to release the seeds and the cone falls to the ground. Small male cones are produced each spring and make pollen in sacs attached to a cluster of scales.

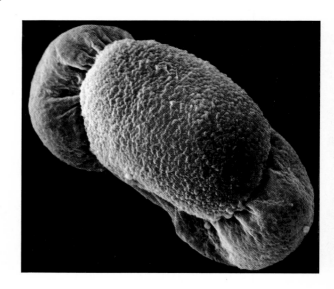

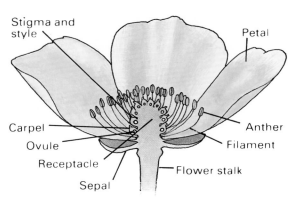

Stigma and style · Petal · Carpel · Anther · Ovule · Filament · Receptacle · Flower stalk · Sepal

Young female Catkins · Turkey oak · Female flower · Ripe female flowers look like cones · Ripe catkins (male flowers) · Common alder · Male catkins

Above: Section through a buttercup flower to show the various structures inside.
Right: Tree flowers are often arranged in long bunches called *catkins.*

A Closer Look at Flowers

Flowers are probably the most amazing structures in the plant world. Despite the huge variety of shapes, sizes and colors, they are all made of the same parts.

All flowers are basically four rings of specially modified leaves attached to a stalk. The bottom ring is made of sepals and is called the *calyx*, which means bud scales. Above the calyx is a ring of petals known as the *corolla*, which means crown. Above the petals is a ring of wand-like *stamens* called the *androecium*, which means male parts. Pollen is produced on the tips of the stamens, which are called *anthers*. Above the androecium, right in the middle of the flower, are the *carpels*. All the carpels together are known as the *gynoecium*, which means female parts. Each carpel has a sticky tip called a *stigma* on top of a stalk called a *style*. Below the style is a hollow structure called an *ovary*, which contains the egg cell inside an *ovule*.

There are all sorts of variations on this basic plan. For example, some of the different parts of a flower may be joined together or some parts may be missing, as in unisex flowers. Flowers of the other sex may be on the same plant (as in hazel) or different plants (as in holly).

Above: A rich variety of flowers can be found in Alpine meadows.
Below: The pollen grains of four flowering plants seen under a high-power electron microscope. From left to right: bindweed, timothy grass, lettuce, and yellow water lily.

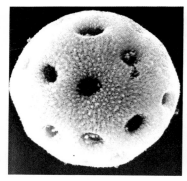
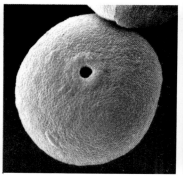
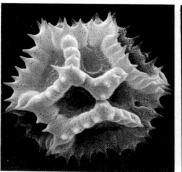
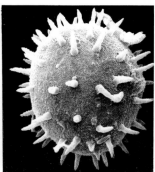

Pollen on the Move

Pollen grains have to make their way to a *stigma* (one of the female parts of a flower) if a new seed is to develop. The transfer of pollen from an anther to a stigma is called *pollination*. The pollen of some flowers travels on the wind. Other flowers rely on insects or other animals to pick up their pollen and carry it from flower to flower.

Some plants can make seeds with pollen from the same plant or even from the same flower. This is called *self-pollination*. Garden peas always make seeds this way. Other plants, such as willow-herb (fireweed) only make seeds with their own pollen if they do not receive pollen from another plant.

Most plants do not self-pollinate because stronger, more varied plants are produced if two different plants breed together. Self-pollination is prevented in several different ways. For example, the stigma and anthers may ripen at different times or in different flowers, or the stigma may have a special chemical system to spot unwanted pollen grains and stop them growing. Some plants, such as dandelions, can make seeds without any pollen. This is called *apomixis*.

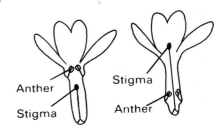

Male and female holly flowers grow on different trees. This is an extreme way of avoiding self-pollination.

Only female holly trees have berries.

Primroses are pollinated by bees. Bees pick up pollen from the anthers of one plant and may carry it to the stigma of another plant.

Anther | Stigma
Stigma | Anther

Some primrose flowers have their anthers high up and their stigmas low down, while others have their stigmas high up and their anthers low down. This helps to prevent pollen grains from reaching the stigma on the same plant.

INSECT POLLINATION

1. Flowers relatively large with brightly colored petals, scent and nectar.

2. Anthers firmly fixed to filaments and held inside flower where insects might brush against them.

3. Not much pollen produced. Pollen grains large with rough surface. Grains may stick together in clumps.

4. Flat and sticky stigmas held inside flower where insects may brush against them.

WIND POLLINATION

1. Flowers small and often green. Petals small or missing altogether. No scent or nectar.

2. Anthers loosely fixed to filaments and held outside flower so that any breeze can shake the pollen from them.

3. Lots of pollen produced. Pollen grains small with a smooth surface. Grains do not stick together.

4. Long, feathery stigmas held outside flower to catch pollen from the air.

Above: These birch tree catkins are made up of lots of male flowers growing together on a long stalk. The flowers on the catkins open in spring before the leaves emerge from the buds on the tree. This means the pollen stands more chance of being blown away by the wind. One birch catkin can produce over five million pollen grains.

Below: The annual meadowgrass has a tall spike of flowers held above the leaves. The anthers dangle loosely outside the male flowers so the wind will blow their pollen away. The feathery stigmas catch the pollen from other flowers.

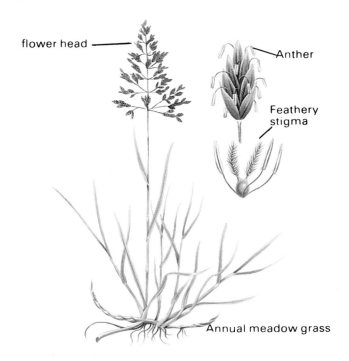

flower head

Anther

Feathery stigma

Annual meadow grass

Blown by the Wind

Many flowers are wind-pollinated, for example many trees, grasses and some common weeds such as stinging nettle. Launching pollen on the wind is a risky business for a plant because it is a matter of chance whether the pollen reaches its destination. So the plant needs to produce a lot of pollen to make sure some of it stands a chance of landing on the stigma of another plant. For example, one male plant of dog's mercury (a small plant that grows in European woods) can produce about 1.3 billion pollen grains!

Apart from producing lots of pollen, the shape of wind-pollinated flowers and the way the different parts of the flowers are arranged helps their pollen to be blown away by the wind and the pollen of other flowers to be trapped on their stigmas. They do not need the large colorful petals, scent or nectar (a sweet food) that other flowers use to attract insects and other animals to carry their pollen. (Turn to pages 72 and 73 to find out about flowers that are pollinated by animals.)

Instead, wind-pollinated flowers are usually small and grouped in a long flower stalk called an *inflorescence*. In some plants, such as grasses, the inflorescence is held high above the leaves but in others, such as tree catkins, it dangles below them. The anthers are large and hang outside the flower on long stalks called *filaments*. Even a slight breeze can shake the flower so that pollen is released.

The pollen grains themselves are small and light, with a smooth, streamlined surface, which helps them to travel easily on the air currents. There are records of pollen traveling as far as 3,000 miles (5,000 kilometers) – far enough to cross the United States at its widest point. To catch the pollen arriving from other flowers, the stigmas hang outside the flower and are large, branched and often feathery. You may have seen the long tassels on a corn stalk.

Hay Fever

People who suffer from hay fever are allergic to pollen in the air. In the spring and summer, when plants are producing clouds of pollen, these people sneeze and their eyes and noses run almost as if they had a cold. Sometimes they also have difficulty breathing. Tablets or injections may help to relieve the symptoms.

71

Pollen Messengers

Many flowers rely on animal messengers, especially insects, to carry their pollen from one flower to another. This sort of flower is easy to recognize. The petals are usually large and brightly colored. They may be scented and produce a sweet food called *nectar* for their pollen carriers to eat. The anthers are firmly fixed on top of strong filaments and are held in just the right place for pollen to brush off onto an animal visiting the flower. The pollen grains may even be rough and sticky to cling to an animal's body. (In many orchids, the pollen grains stick together in clumps so that they can be carried in a sort of parcel.) The stigmas are held where a visiting animal cannot avoid touching them.

Insect Visitors

Insects are often attracted to a flower by its color. Yellow, blue and white are particularly popular. Markings on the petals may act much like the guiding lights on an airfield, showing the insect where to land and which direction to move in. Some of these colors and markings are invisible to us because we cannot see ultraviolet light.

An interesting smell also attracts insect visitors. The sweet scent of flowers such as lavender and honeysuckle advertises nectar, which is the favorite food of many insects. Honeybees turn nectar into honey. It would take one bee eight years to make a pound of honey.

Not all plants smell pleasant – some smell revolting. Many flies feed on rotting meat and some flowers can reproduce the smell perfectly to trick insects into visiting them. The *Stapelia* flower not only smells like decaying flesh but looks like it as well. It has red petals that look like meat and hairs around the edge that look like fur. The disguise is so good that female flies lay their eggs on the flowers, just as they do on a real carcass.

An insect does not need any special skills to be a pollen messenger. Clambering about inside a flower is often enough to get dusted in pollen. Some insects actually eat some of the pollen. Bees collect pollen and feed it to their developing young. But there is usually enough pollen left over to be carried to other flowers. One

Above: Honeybees scrape off the pollen dust that clings to their bodies and pack it into pollen baskets made of stiff bristles on their thighs. They use the pollen to feed their young and only a small amount of it pollinates flowers. But bees do pollinate flowers as they search for their favorite food, nectar. Watch a bee as it collects nectar and try to see which flowers it visits most often.

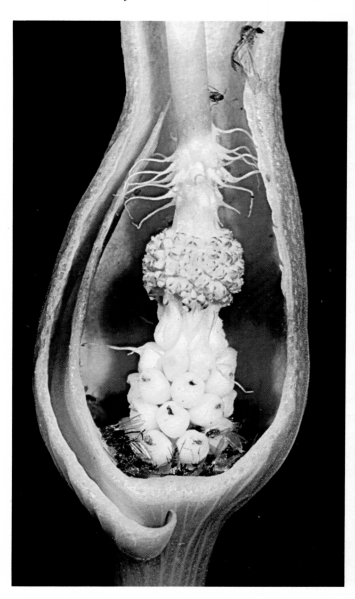

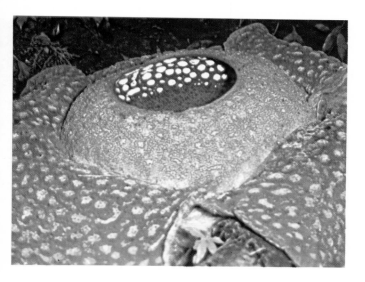

Rafflesia is the largest flower in the world and measures about three feet (one meter) across. It attracts flies to its huge petals which look and smell like rotting meat. As they clamber about on the flower, the flies deliver and collect pollen. Only the flower grows above ground. The rest of the plant is a network of threads that grows inside the roots of a vine.

Left: The arum lily lures flies into its flower chamber with warmth and a powerful smell. The flies climb past the unripe anthers and onto the stigmas, where some of the pollen they are carrying rubs off. They are trapped for about three days until the downward-pointing hairs shrivel. Then the anthers open to dust the insects with pollen and they climb out of their prison.

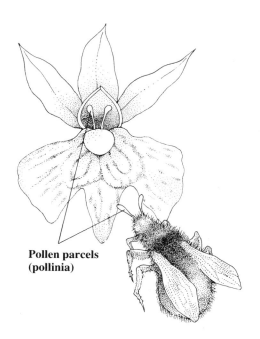

Pollen parcels (pollinia)

Orchid flowers have special "pollen parcels" called *pollinia* instead of anthers. The pollinia consist of clusters of pollen grains stuck firmly together in a club-shaped structure. At the base of each pollinia is a sticky pad which can glue it to the head of an insect that visits the flower. The bee in the picture above has two pollinia stuck to its head. These may fertilize the unpollinated orchid flower it is about to land on. The bee may also pick up more pollinia from this flower before it leaves.

species of myrtle produces two sorts of pollen – one that pollinates flowers and one that is particularly tasty and more likely to be eaten by insects.

Plants that do not have much pollen to spare guide insects to just the right place. Often the weight of the insect on the petals is enough to trigger a flick of the anther so that pollen is smeared onto its head, back or abdomen. You can see this happening if you watch a bee landing on an *Antirrhinum* (snapdragon) flower. As the bee pushes the petal down, the anther jerks forward and showers pollen onto its back.

Special Insect Flowers

Some flowers have developed unusual ways of making sure their pollen always goes to the right sort of flower so that no pollen is wasted. These flowers are tailor-made to suit a particular insect.

Some orchid flowers look, smell and feel very much like a particular species of female insect. Different species of orchid look like different insects – you can see one that looks like a bee on page 23. A male insect of the same species is attracted to the flower and tries to mate with it.

As he does so, a parcel of pollen sticks to him. He then flies from flower to flower and as he tries to mate with each of them he collects and delivers pollen.

The only insect that can get pollen from the South American *yucca* plant is a moth with a tongue that curves in just the right way to pick up pollen. The moth packs the pollen into a ball and flies off with it to another flower. She lays her eggs through the wall of the ovary in this flower and then climbs up to the stigma and fixes the pollen ball there. Seeds can then develop in the ovary along with the moth caterpillars. So the yucca provides a nursery for the moth and the moth pollinates the yucca.

Bird and Bat Messengers

In tropical countries, some flowers are pollinated by birds. They produce a particularly rich nectar for their special visitors. A few tropical flowers are also pollinated by bats. Bats are color-blind so the flowers are often rather dull colors. They open in the evening as the bats start to fly and attract them with an interesting smell. As the bat laps up nectar with its long tongue, pollen dust is showered onto its body.

73

A common poppy flower, with two seed capsules in the background. Each poppy flower can produce hundreds of seeds.

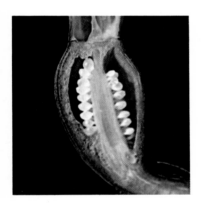

Left: Cross section of the ovary of a daffodil. The ovules grow in rows around the center of the ovary. Each ovule can develop into a seed if it is fertilized by pollen. Try slicing open the ovaries of different flowers to see how the ovules are arranged.

Making Seeds

When the pollen carried by the wind or an animal messenger lands on the stigma of a flower, it has to make its way to the ovule before a seed can develop. It soaks up sugary liquid from the stigma and a tube grows out of the pollen grain, down the style and into the ovary. It enters the ovule through a tiny hole called the *micropyle*.

Inside the ovule, the tip of the pollen tube breaks open. It releases a nucleus that joins with the nucleus of the egg cell. This process is called *fertilization* and the new cell that is formed is the start of a seed. Many pollen tubes may start to grow down the style but only one will fertilize each egg cell. In flowering plants, a second nucleus comes out of the pollen tube and joins with another female nucleus in the ovule. This may then grow to become a food supply (called *endosperm*) for the developing seed.

The petals, stamens, style and stigma are no longer needed. They wither away and usually drop off. The sepals sometimes stay and may develop to protect the seeds. The hard green lump at one end of an orange is the remains of the sepals.

Below: A simplified diagram of a single carpel in an ovary after fertilization. A pollen tube grows down to the ovary from a pollen grain that lands on the stigma. It usually enters the ovule through a small hole called the *micropyle*. The tip of the pollen tube breaks open and releases two male nuclei. One of these fuses with the female nucleus in the ovule to become the first cell of a new seed.

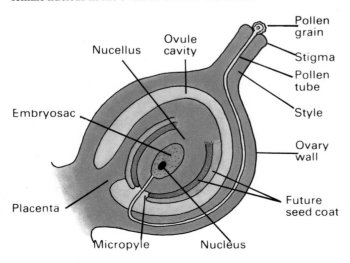

74

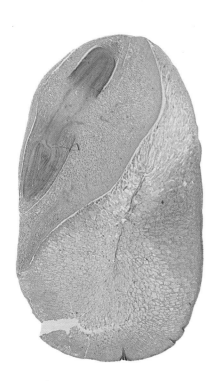

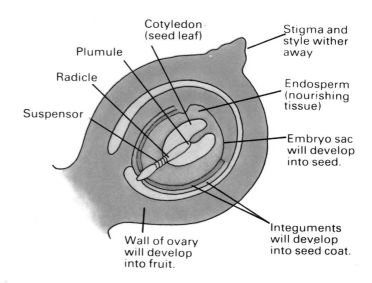

Above: A simplified diagram of a seed forming in one of the carpels inside an ovary. You can see the miniature plant developing in the middle. It has a shoot (*plumule*), a root (*radicle*) and two seed leaves, which are called *cotyledons*. The cotyledons contain enough food to feed the plant until it can make its own food.

Left: Cross section of a corn Kernel to show the developing embryo.

From Seed to Fruit

The seed ripens with food sent to it from the leaves. It develops a miniature shoot (called a *plumule*) and a miniature root (called a *radicle*) and one or two seed leaves called *cotyledons*. The cotyledons may be a rich food supply for the new plant. Grasses, cereals and narrow-leaved plants such as tulips have one cotyledon and are called *monocotyledons*. All other flowering plants have two cotyledons and are called *dicotyledons*.

The seed grows a waterproof coat (called a *testa*), which helps to protect it from pests and diseases. If you split open a broad bean you can see the miniature plant inside. The two large lobes are the cotyledons and between them are the tiny root and shoot. At one end is a scar (called a *hilum*) where the seed was joined to the bean pod (ovary wall). You may also be able to find the hole where the pollen tube entered. A bean seed has no endosperm, just large cotyledons. You can see endosperm in the seed of a grain plant, such as corn.

When the seed is fully grown, it becomes hard as it dries out, ready to survive in difficult conditions. By this time the ovary wall has developed into a *fruit*. Some fruits, such as plums and cherries, have one large seed but other fruits, such as grapes and tomatoes, contain several small seeds. A blackberry is several small fruits joined together in a structure called a *drupe*. Each pip is a seed. In a strawberry, however, each pip is a whole fruit. The red, fleshy part is the swollen center of the flower. Apples and pears are fleshy flower stalks that grow around the ovary and join the ovary wall. Many structures called vegetables (such as squash and green peppers) are really fruits because they contain seeds.

When do Plants Make Seeds?

Plants do not make seeds all the time. Some, such as the poppy, make seeds at the end of one growing season and then die. They are called *annuals* and survive the winter cold or a dry season only as seeds. Other plants, such as the carrot, grow for two years before they flower, produce seeds and die. They are called *biennials*. In their first year, biennials store food underground to help them survive the following winter or dry season. Plants that grow for several years are called *perennials*. Some perennials, such as many trees, make flowers and seeds every year. But others only do so from time to time. Most trees can live for hundreds of years. Plants that reproduce by runners, such as strawberries, can live indefinitely.

Above: The fruits of a cut-leaved cranesbill plant. On the left of the picture are some unripe fruits. When the fruits are ripe, they explode and curl up, as you can see to the right of the picture. This throws the seeds away from the parent plant.

Above: A squirting cucumber plant with flowers and unripe fruits. When these are ripe, they will burst open to shoot the seeds out. They may travel for several yards before they fall to the ground. If they land in a suitable place, they may grow into new plants.

Right: The Indian balsam plant has capsules which suddenly twist open to throw out the seeds quite violently. A slight touch is enough to trigger a mini-explosion that shoots the seeds away from the fruit. You can see how this happens in the diagram below (to the right).

Below left: A vetch pod suddenly splits and throws out the seeds.

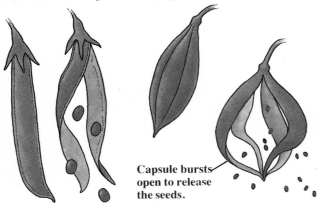

Capsule bursts open to release the seeds.

Spreading Seeds

If a seed sprouts too near its parent, it may not get enough light, water and minerals to grow. So once a plant has made seeds, it must spread them to make sure they have a good start in life. Seeds travel away from the parent plant in four ways. They may be thrown out by the plant itself or be carried away by the wind, water or passing animals. If a fruit splits open when it is ripe and shoots its seeds out, it is called a *dehiscent* fruit. If the seeds are released by some other means, it is called an *indehiscent* fruit.

Catapults and Guns
Some plants sow their own seeds with the help of springs and catapults. When gorse pods are ripe, the two halves suddenly twist apart, flinging the seeds in all directions. Many fruits shoot out their seeds if something touches them. For pennycress, the weight of a raindrop is enough to eject the seeds. One of the strangest fruits is the squirting cucumber. It squirts all its seeds out in a stream through a sort of plug hole. The seeds may land several yards away.

Wind Transport
The wind can carry seeds for many miles – an average journey for a dandelion seed is about 6 miles (10 kilometers). Orchid seeds are so small they drift like dust in the air. Many seeds have

some sort of wings to help them glide or spin through the air. Most conifer seeds are spread this way as are the familiar spinning "keys" of sycamore and maple. Scabious and thrift seeds develop little frills and float on the wind like shuttlecocks. Tumbleweed plants scatter their own seeds by uprooting themselves and rolling along in the wind.

Water Transport

Not many seeds travel by water. Those that do are mostly from water plants. They have a waterproof skin and some sort of float. In the Indian lotus plant, the whole woody seed head breaks off and floats like a raft.

Animal Transport

Many plants depend on animals to spread their seeds. Some fruits and seeds have hooks to stick to the coat of a passing animal. They may be carried long distances before they are brushed off by the undergrowth. Other fruits have bright colors and sometimes have a shiny surface to attract animals to eat them. The seeds have tough walls so they pass through the animal unharmed and come out in the droppings. If a seed lands in a suitable place, it may grow into a new plant – with the help of natural fertilizer in the droppings. Nuts may be spread by animals that store them for the winter. The animals often collect more than they need and the left-overs can grow in the spring.

Below: A female blackbird eating hawthorn berries. Birds eat juicy berries and either spit out the seeds or pass them out with their droppings. The seeds can then grow into new plants. Some seeds have to pass through an animal's system before they sprout.

SEEDS ON YOUR FEET

Animals often pick up seeds on their feet and carry them away from the parent plant. How many seeds do you pick up on a muddy walk? Try the experiment below to find out.

1. Scrape the mud off your boots or shoes into a tray or flowerpot of sterilized compost. You can sterilize the compost by baking it in the oven. This kills any living seeds in it.

2. Water the tray and cover it with glass or plastic. (This will stop any seeds from the air getting in.) Keep it moist and warm.

3. Watch to see how many seeds sprout in the tray. They can only have come from the mud you brought home on your shoes.

Below: Some seeds, such as the dandelion (left) are blown away by the wind. Others, such as sanicle (right) have hooks or barbs which catch in the fur of passing animals.

A seed of sanicle attached to the fur of an animal with its tiny hooks.

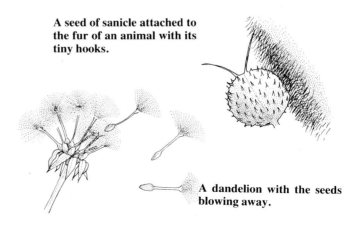

A dandelion with the seeds blowing away.

How Plants Grow

Seeds are survival kits against cold and dry conditions. They do not usually grow as soon as they land on the soil but remain dormant for days, months or even years. They begin to grow only when they have enough warmth, water and oxygen. This process is called *germination*.

A seed begins to germinate by taking in water. It swells up and the seed coat splits. The root appears first and grows down into the soil. Then the shoot begins to grow upward. In flowering plants, roots grow down and shoots grow up – no matter which way up the seed is planted. The stored food in the cotyledons or endosperm helps the seed to grow until the new plant develops leaves to make its own food.

In plants such as the broad bean, the cotyledons always stay underground. This sort of germination is called *hypogeal*, which means "under the soil." In plants such as the sunflower, the cotyledons are pushed above the ground and become the first green leaves. This sort of germination is called *epigeal*, which means "above the soil."

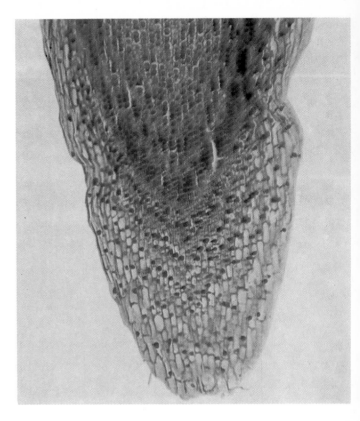

Above: Part of an onion root under a high-power microscope. In the tip of the root (behind the root cap) the cells are dividing over and over again so that the root grows longer. This region is called a *meristem* (growing tip). You can see the nuclei (dark circles) in the center of the cells. The root cap protects the meristem as it pushes through the soil.

Left: A coconut seedling germinating. The seedling cannot make its own food until the first green leaves develop. Until then it depends on food stored inside the seed.

The growth of roots and shoots is controlled by chemical messengers called *auxins*. Auxins are similar to the hormones that control animal growth. In a shoot, auxins are produced at the tip and travel downward to make the cells behind the tip grow. Light destroys the auxin so the shoot grows more on the side *away from* the light. This makes the shoot curve toward the light. In a root, auxin slows the growth of cells. It gathers in the cells on the lower side of the root. The cells on the *upper side* grow more so the root curves downward. These movements of the shoot and root are called *tropisms* and they help the plant to get the light and water it needs to grow.

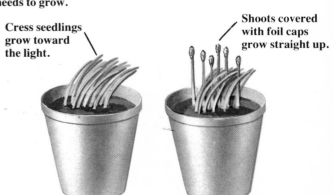

Cress seedlings grow toward the light.

Shoots covered with foil caps grow straight up.

Growing Longer and Thicker

Plants, unlike animals, continue to grow throughout their lives. Growth takes place in certain regions of the plant called *meristems*. In a young plant the meristems are at the tip of the roots and shoots. The cells continually divide and expand to push the shoot up and the root down.

Plants that do not survive from year to year above the ground grow mostly by increasing in length like this. But woody plants, such as trees and shrubs, get thicker as well as longer. As this takes place after they have increased in length, it is called *secondary thickening*.

The meristem that produces this outward growth is called *vascular cambium*. In a young woody plant, this consists of small groups of cells between the xylem and phloem in each vascular bundle of a root or shoot. These link up to form a ring of cambium separating the xylem from the phloem. Then the cambium cells produce a thick ring of new xylem tissue (wood) on the inside and a thin ring of new phloem tissue on the outside. Another meristem, called *cork cambium*, is formed just under the surface of the stem. This produces the thick-walled cork cells in bark.

Above: The ancient eastern tradition of *bonsai* has produced this miniature *Pinus thunbergii* tree. Bonsai trees grow from normal trees but do not get enough food and water to grow to a normal size. Their shoots are pruned and their roots trimmed so they remain as dwarfs. It takes great skill to produce a bonsai tree and may take many years to create a tree like this. Some bonsai trees are hundreds of years old.

Secondary growth takes place in summer but stops in winter. The rings you can see in a tree trunk mark the start of each year's growth. They are called *annual rings*. The cambium forms large xylem cells in spring (when growing conditions are good) and small xylem cells toward the end of summer. The rings show up where the small cells of one year stop and the large cells of the next year begin. You can tell the age of a tree by counting the annual rings.

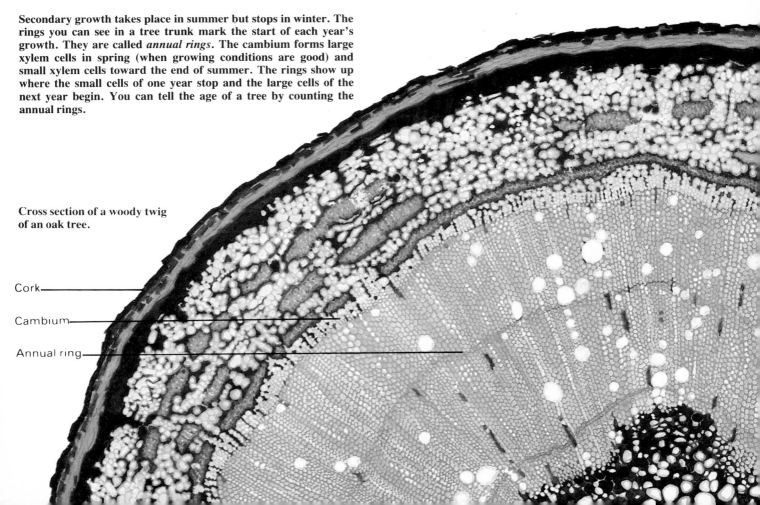

Cross section of a woody twig of an oak tree.

Cork

Cambium

Annual ring

Wild daffodils growing in the country.

Left: Cross section of daffodil bulb to show the swollen leaf bases wrapped around a short underground stem.
Food made in the leaves is sent down to the leaf bases to be stored during the summer. New bulbs develop from side buds that grow out from the main stem.

New bulb   Parent bulb

Below: Cuckoo pint stores food in a swollen underground stem called a *corm*. Strong roots pull the corm back down into the soil.

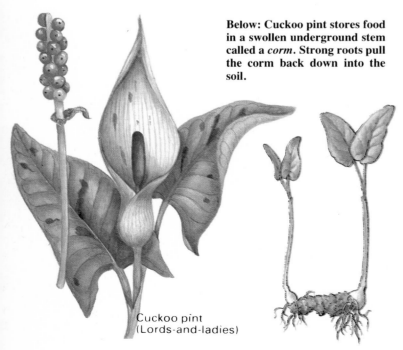

Cuckoo pint
(Lords-and-ladies)

New Plants from Old

Some flowering plants can produce a new plant from a small part of themselves as well as (or instead of) reproducing by seeds. A small section of the plant, such as part of a stem or leaf, can replace the missing parts and develop into a new individual. This is known as *vegetative reproduction*.

People take advantage of this to reproduce their house or garden plants. They cut off a healthy young shoot and plant it in some fresh soil. If roots grow, the cutting may become established as a new plant. New begonias and African violets can even be grown from the leaves.

Many plants survive from year to year by means of vegetative reproduction. They form storage organs, such as bulbs, in which they store the food they make during the summer. The storage organ remains in the ground over the winter after the rest of the plant has died. A new plant grows out of it the following year, using the energy in the stored food. This allows woodland plants that grow from bulbs to develop leaves and flowers early in the year before the leaves on the trees cut out the sunlight they need to make food.

A bulb has buds (just like any stem) so a new bulb may sprout from the side of the old one

Bryophyllum produces tiny plantlets along its leaves.

during the growing season. Gardeners often dig up the new bulbs and plant them separately, ready for the following year.

Other storage organs may also be a way of reproducing as well as helping the plant to survive the winter. Some plants, such as irises, store food in swollen underground stems called *rhizomes*. Rhizomes can become quite large, as the old stems last for several years. Plants, such as the potato have slender rhizomes with swollen tips, called *tubers*. The actual potato is a tuber. If you look at a potato you can see it is a stem because it has traces of the leaves and buds – these are the "eyes." Each eye can grow into a new plant using the food stored in the potato.

Buttercups and strawberry plants produce long, spindly stems, called *runners*, above the ground. At the end of the runner, a new plant begins to grow and take root, using the food passed along from the parent plant. When the plant is big enough to make its own food, the runner withers and dies, leaving the new plant growing by itself.

A blackberry bush is really many blackberry plants made by the stems arching over and taking root where they touch the soil. Unlike the strawberry, the stems that produce new plants do not die but continue to grow, making the bush more and more tangled. Gardeners sometimes produce new bushes by bending over a young branch on a shrub and pushing it into the soil so that roots will grow.

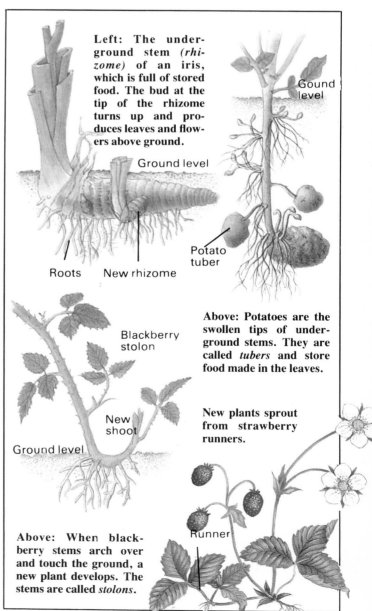

Left: The underground stem (*rhizome*) of an iris, which is full of stored food. The bud at the tip of the rhizome turns up and produces leaves and flowers above ground.

Ground level

Roots   New rhizome

Gound level

Potato tuber

Above: Potatoes are the swollen tips of underground stems. They are called *tubers* and store food made in the leaves.

New plants sprout from strawberry runners.

Blackberry stolon

New shoot

Ground level

Above: When blackberry stems arch over and touch the ground, a new plant develops. The stems are called *stolons*.

Runner

Algae, Mosses and Ferns

Algae, mosses and ferns do not have flowers and so cannot make seeds. Instead they produce *spores*, which develop inside a structure called a *fruiting body*. Spores are small and light and float on the air or sometimes on water. If they land in a suitable place they may grow into new plants.

Algae

Algae alive today include the seaweeds and microscopic forms that turn pondwater green. Some algae can reproduce simply by splitting into two. Others grow from fragments of the parent plant or sprout from the end of long runners produced by the parent plant. Some algae grow from spores produced when two cells join together. Many algae can reproduce in more than one way.

Mosses

The leafy moss plant grows from a spore that has landed in a suitable spot. The tips of the shoots grow special sex cells – female egg cells on some shoots, male cells on others. A male cell swims to an egg cell and fertilizes it. The egg cell does not grow into a moss plant but makes spores instead. From the fertilized egg cell a stalk grows

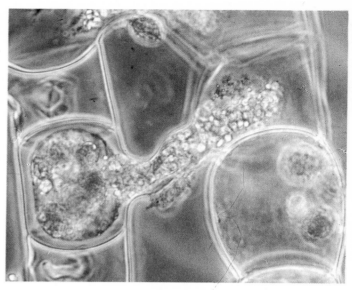

Above: Part of two strands of an alga called *Spirogyra* as it appears under the microscope. Spirogyra can produce a special sort of spore when the contents of one cell pass through a tube to join with the contents of a cell in a different strand. The spore is protected by a thick coat and can survive difficult conditions.

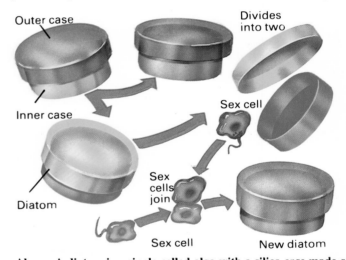

Above: A diatom is a single-celled alga with a silica case made of two halves. When the cell divides, the two halves of the case pull apart and each half quickly makes a new case to fit inside the old one. When the cases get very small, sex cells are produced and they fuse to form a new diatom.

Below: The life cycle of a common moss, such as *Funaria*. The leafy plant produces male and female cells, which join together to grow into a case containing spores. This remains attached to the leafy plant. Spores are released into the air and grow into a new leafy moss plant if they land on a suitable patch of ground.

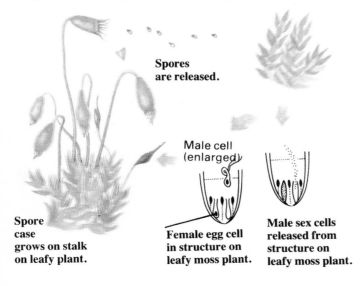

Spores are released.

Male cell (enlarged)

Spore case grows on stalk on leafy plant.

Female egg cell in structure on leafy moss plant.

Male sex cells released from structure on leafy moss plant.

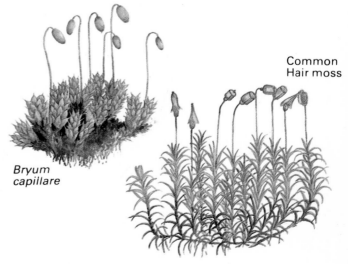

Bryum capillare

Common Hair moss

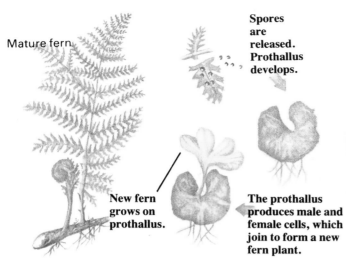

Mature fern

Spores are released. Prothallus develops.

New fern grows on prothallus.

The prothallus produces male and female cells, which join to form a new fern plant.

Above: The life cycle of the common fern, *Dryopteris*. It reproduces in two stages, like the moss on page 82. Look for the brown spore cases under fern fronds.

Below: The fronds of male fern unfolding in spring. This fern grows in woods, mountainsides and home gardens. The stem is underground.

upward with a *capsule* full of spores at the top. When the capsule is ripe, it releases the spores.

Ferns

Ferns, like mosses, develop in two stages. In mosses the main plant is the one that produces male and female cells. In ferns the main plant is the one that produces spores. Fern spores develop in brown spore cases called *sporangia* under some of the leaves (*fronds*). The sporangia usually occur in round or long, thin clusters called *sori* (singular *sorus*) but in some ferns they are evenly distributed over part or all of the underside of the frond.

When the spores are ripe, the sori split open in dry air and the spores are flicked clear of the plant. They look like dust to the naked eye but under the microscope it is possible to see patterns such as spines, pores and ridges on the surface of the spores. The spores need damp conditions to germinate. They grow into a thin, heart-shaped leaf called a *prothallus* (plural *prothalli*) on the surface of the ground. Most prothalli are less than half an inch (one centimeter) long.

Minute roots and microscopic sex organs grow underneath the prothallus. Sex cells develop inside the sex organs. In the dark and the damp, the male cells swim to the female cells and fertilize them. The new cell grows into a fern plant, which lives on the prothallus until it is established. It grows so slowly that it may take a year before a new fern plant appears.

Below: This liverwort is best known as a weed in greenhouses where it grows on the soil in flowerpots. Liverworts reproduce by spores in a similar way to their relatives, the mosses. New plants can also grow from buds sprouting from the parent plant.

A liverwort called *Marchantia polymorpha*.

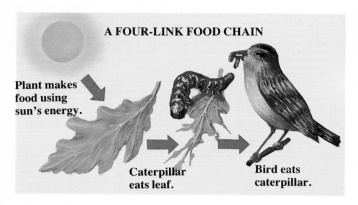

A FOUR-LINK FOOD CHAIN

Plant makes food using sun's energy.

Caterpillar eats leaf.

Bird eats caterpillar.

Above: The sun's energy is trapped by plants, which are in turn eaten by animals. This is called a food chain. Food chains link together to form food webs because most animals have several kinds of food.

**Above: White rhinoceroses have ridged teeth and broad mouths for cropping grass. They graze on the savanna plains of Africa.
Below: A sea anemone feeding on a prawn. Sea anemones have stinging cells to paralyze their prey.**

Finding Food

Living things obtain the food they need in a variety of different ways. Green plants make their own food from chemicals they take in from the air, soil and water. Animals, however, cannot make food. They have to take it in ready-made by eating plants or other animals.

Plant-eaters are known as *herbivores*. They include animals such as horses, sheep and rabbits that graze on grass, as well as less familiar animals, such as shellfish called limpets, which feed on the seaweed growing on rocks.

Herbivores are eaten in turn by meat-eating animals, which are called *carnivores*. These include the lions, wolves and other big carnivores, which can kill herbivores the size of a horse. Small carnivores such as sea snails drill holes through the shells of shellfish and suck out the soft insides. Carnivores may also eat other carnivores. For example, killer whales hunt seals, which feed on fish. Some animals, called *omnivores*, eat both plants and animals.

The dead bodies of plants and animals and the waste substances they produce also provide food for other creatures. For instance, vultures tear flesh from dead animals, certain beetles feed on dung and earthworms extract nutrients from rotting leaves. Soil contains tiny organisms called decay bacteria which break down dead plant and animal material into simple chemicals. These chemicals are sucked up by the roots of plants.

Thus, every creature in the natural world is linked with another which either eats it or is eaten by it, forming a *food chain*. Many of these food chains are connected, as most animals feed on more than one kind of plant or other animal. So the chains themselves link up to form a *food web* – the web of life.

Hunting Tactics

Many hunters have special features that help them to find food. Owls have huge eyes and very sensitive ears that help them to detect their prey at night. A flying bat squeaks and listens for the echoes bounced back off flying moths. This helps the bat to home in on the moths and snap them up.

Some hunters chase their prey over long distances. A pack of wolves may pursue a caribou for miles. When it tires they run in for the kill. Big cats, such as lions, prefer to creep up stealthily and make a short, sharp rush to finish the animal off. Certain other creatures set traps or lures and wait for prey to come to them. An insect called an ant lion digs a little pit in sand and feeds on the ants that tumble in. The deep-sea angler fish grows what looks like a fishing line baited with wriggling worms. When fish swim up to seize the "worms" the angler fish swallows them up.

Teeth, beaks or claws are the main weapons for many hunters, but a few make use of tools. Egyptian vultures drop lumps of rock on ostrich eggs to break open the shells and sea otters crack open clams by bashing them with stones.

Above: The feathery tentacles of the fanworm wave in the sea currents to trap tiny particles of food. Fanworms live in protective tubes made of small stones or sand grains stuck together. They build up the tubes as they grow.

Below: Some animals feed on dead and decaying matter. Dung beetles shape dung into a ball and then usually work in pairs to push the ball along until they find a suitable place to bury it. The female lays one or more eggs in the ball of dung and the larvae feed on it as they grow.

Below: An egg-eating snake can unhinge its jaws so that they stretch wide enough to allow it to swallow a whole egg. This may take up to 15 minutes for a large egg. Sharp bones in the snake's throat crush the egg shell. The snake swallows the contents of the egg and spits out the crushed shell.

Staying Alive

Many animals and plants have special characteristics to help them avoid ending up as another animal's dinner.

Running Away

Long-legged grazing or browsing animals can outrun most of their enemies. A herd of antelopes can outgallop a lion, if the antelopes have a start. Rabbits can run faster than most dogs. If speedy creatures get caught, it is probably because they are either old, very young, ill or taken by surprise.

Escaping somewhere out of reach of enemies is another way to stay alive. Agile monkeys and mountain goats can outclimb leopards. Scared terrapins plunge into a nearby pond. Frightened rabbits dash down burrows.

Armor and Thick Skin

Slow movers defend themselves in other ways. Turtles and crabs hide their soft bodies inside hard outer shells. In the same way that thick bark protects trees from the teeth of browsing mammals such as deer, animals such as elephants grow very thick skin which even a lion's teeth find hard to bite through.

Clever Camouflage

Camouflage is another life-saver. Camouflaged animals have shapes or colors like those of their surroundings. For instance, a flounder looks like the patch of sand it lies on. Many newborn deer are brown with pale spots. When they lie down in a wood, they look just like a patch of bracken lit by sunlight.

Above: A grass snake sometimes pretends to be dead when it is attacked. This may fool its attacker into leaving it alone.
Below: Armadillos are small "armor-plated" mammals that roll up into a ball when attacked. Their "armor" protects them.

Above: The wobbegong is an Australian shark, which is camouflaged by a fringe around its head.
Below: Some plants have swollen leaves that look like pebbles. This disguise probably helps them to escape being eaten.

Threatened musk oxen form a ring around their small defenseless young to protect them from wolves.

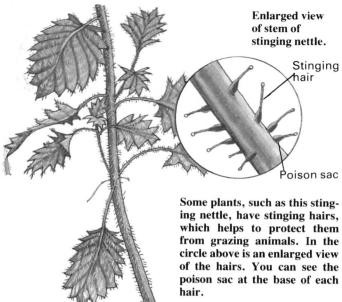
Enlarged view of stem of stinging nettle.

Stinging hair

Poison sac

Some plants, such as this stinging nettle, have stinging hairs, which helps to protect them from grazing animals. In the circle above is an enlarged view of the hairs. You can see the poison sac at the base of each hair.

Certain creatures do not just match the colors of their surroundings, they match the shapes of objects around them as well. You can easily mistake a looper caterpillar for a short, brown twig, while some butterflies look just like real dead leaves. But all these camouflaged animals stay safe and hidden only while they keep quite still. The moment they move, they may be discovered and eaten.

Weapons and Poisons

Not all animals freeze, run, hide or rely on armor to protect them when they are threatened. Some have formidable weapons of defense. Sea urchins look like small pincushions bristling with long, sharp pins. Larger animals such as hedgehogs and porcupines also have protective spines. A hedgehog curls up into a spiny ball when attacked but a porcupine will back into its enemy and drive its long, sharp quills into its attacker's legs or face. Spines also help to protect plants from grazing animals.

Claws, hooves, horns and teeth are among the best weapons of defense. Africa's rhinoceroses and buffalo put down their great horned heads and charge an enemy. An ostrich can kill a person with a powerful kick from one of its clawed feet. Even a cornered rat can give a painful bite.

Some plants and animals protect themselves with poisons. These may just make them taste so unpleasant that animals avoid eating them. Or they may be strong poisons that can kill their attackers. Bees can kill other insects with their poisoned stings and many frogs, toads and salamanders have deadly poisons in their skin. Such poisonous or unpleasant-tasting animals are mostly brightly colored as a warning to would-be predators to keep away.

Yet other creatures just pretend that they are dangerous. Harmless milk snakes look almost identical to deadly coral snakes. Some moths open their wings suddenly to reveal what look like two big, frightening eyes. The frilled lizard spreads its neck frill to make its head appear large and terrifying.

Below: The bright colors on the wings of this tiger moth make it easy for enemies to see. But birds soon learn that this brightly colored insect tastes unpleasant.

Living Together

Certain living creatures form partnerships where animals or plants of different kinds live on, in or with one another. In some cases this helps both partners but sometimes the relationship is entirely one-sided.

Some ferns, mosses and other plants sprout on the branches of jungle trees. (You can see one of these branches in the picture above.) This allows the plants to get more light than if they grew on the dark jungle floor. Falling leaves are caught on the branches where they rot and provide nourishment. Damp air and rain supply plenty of moisture. Plants that grow like this are known as *epiphytes*. They do no real harm to the tree but do not help it either.

A partnership where both partners benefit is known as *symbiosis*. Symbiosis sometimes works with partners of very unequal sizes. A cow has millions of microscopic bacteria inside its food canal (see page 38). The bacteria help to break down grass into simple chemicals the cow can digest, while the cow gives the bacteria food and shelter.

Certain fungi are close partners of conifers and various other trees and shrubs. Fungal threads grow around and inside the tree roots. The fungi take water and minerals from the soil and pass them on to the tree roots. The tree

Above: A sweetlip fish lets a little wrasse swim inside its mouth to feed off parasites. Both fish benefit from this arrangement.
Below: Sea anemones live on the outside of this whelk shell while a hermit crab has made its home inside. The crab is protected by the anemones' stings and the anemones eat any food the crab leaves.

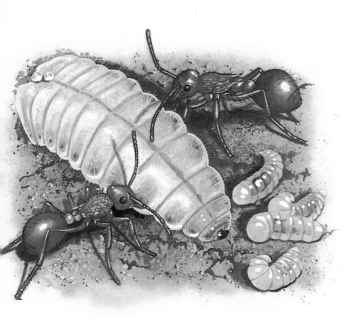

Caterpillars in the butterfly family *Lycaenidae* often live in a form of *symbiosis* (see page 88) with some species of ant. The ants protect the caterpillar inside their nest and the caterpillar may even eat some of the ant larvae. In return, the caterpillars produce a sweet "honey" for the ants to eat.

roots provide sugars in return. This special kind of partnership between the roots of a green plant and a fungus is called a *mycorrhiza*.

Some plant and animal partners cannot exist without each other. They include the flowering plants and insects. Insects such as bees and butterflies get food from flowers. But as they fly from flower to flower they also spread pollen, which fertilizes the flowers' seeds. So without flowers the insects would starve and without insects the flowers could not produce new plants.

There are several famous partnerships between different animals. One involves the oxpecker bird and a rhinoceros. The oxpecker perches on the back of the rhinoceros where it eats flies and ticks and keeps a lookout and gives an early warning of danger. Another animal partnership involves clownfish, which live among the poisonous tentacles of a certain kind of sea anemone in the sea around coral reefs. The anemone does not kill the clownfish because the fish coat their bodies with a special sort of liquid. So the clownfish gain protection from the anemone and in return they may lure other creatures close enough for the anemone to catch. Both the clownfish and the anemone gain from the partnership.

Parasites – All Take and No Give

Parasites are plants or animals that live on or in other kinds of plant or animal, which are called their *hosts*. A parasite takes food from its host but gives nothing back in return.

The largest flower in the world belongs to a parasitic plant called *Rafflesia* (see page 73). Rafflesia's other parts are just slim threads that suck food from the roots and stems of forest plants. Some plants, such as mistletoe, are only half parasites. Mistletoe produces some of its own food but also steals some from the trees it grows on.

Microscopic parasites cause countless illnesses in plants and animals. Viruses give us colds, measles, mumps and other problems (see pages 28-29). Certain fungi cause ringworm, a human skin disease, and other fungi produce rust diseases that damage grain crops.

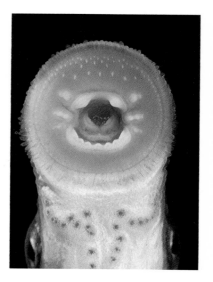

Right: A lamprey's ever-open mouth is a sucker armed with horny teeth. The lamprey fastens its sucker onto a fish and uses tiny teeth on its tongue to rasp away at the fish's flesh. Then the lamprey sucks its victim's blood.

Below: This photograph shows the pink stems of a parasitic plant called dodder growing on a gorse bush. Each young dodder plant puts out suckers that grip another plant. Then the dodder's roots die and it sucks nourishment from its unlucky host.

Partners and Rivals

Male and female animals must meet and mate before they can breed. Each kind of creature has special signals, which help it to attract a partner of the same kind. These signals usually involve the creature's appearance, the sounds it makes or special scents it produces.

Sight Signals

Many male animals are bigger or showier than females of their own kind. Visual (sight) signals help these males attract a mate. For instance, male birds of paradise have much lovelier plumage than their females. They perform acrobatic dances in front of the females. Other kinds of males show off in special ways. Mallard drakes bob their heads. Male newts vibrate their tails. Male Siamese fighting fishes stiffen their splendid fins and waggle their bodies in front of female fighters. A male red-eared terrapin flutters its front legs against the sides of a female's head. Sight signals work even in darkness. Some female insects, such as fireflies, glow brightly at night to attract males.

Sound Signals

Grasshoppers and crickets use sounds as their mating signals. Males rub one part of the body against another. This makes a buzzing or chirruping sound. Males of different species sing different "songs" to attract females of their own kind. It is the same with birds, frogs and toads. The low croak of a male common toad attracts only female common toads.

Above: A small male frog can make a loud sound by blowing up his vocal sac. Male frogs call at mating time to attract a mate.

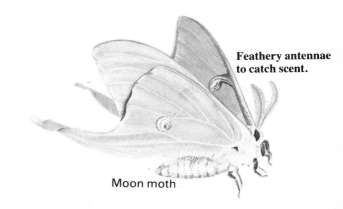

Feathery antennae to catch scent.

Moon moth

Above: A male moth's feathery feelers (antennae) detect tiny particles of scent given off by females of his own kind. He follows the scent trail until he finds the female. Some male moths can find females several miles away.
Below left: Peacocks try to attract peahens by spreading their great fan of feathers and shaking them in a spectacular display as they parade in front of the hens.
Below right: Fireflies attract each other with flashes of light. Different species signal with different patterns of flashes. This helps each individual to recognize others of its own kind.

Peacock displaying to a peahen.

Above: A male and female spoonbill preening each other. Preening is one of the acts of courtship that helps to bring a pair of birds together. After courtship and mating, both birds will work together to build a nest and raise a family.

Below: These male impala are fighting for a herd of females. They clash their heads and horns together in a fierce sounding battle. But after a while, the weaker animal will back off and walk away. Neither animal usually gets seriously hurt. The male that wins the fight will mate with the females.

Scent Signals

For most insects and mammals, scent is the signal that brings males and females together. Usually a special scent produced by the female attracts the male. When a female dog is ready to mate, she gives off a strong scent that attracts male dogs from some distance away.

Fighting for a Mate

Some male animals have to fight other males to win their mates. Rival deer stags fight with their sharp, pointed antlers. They may lock their antlers together in a test of strength. Male fur seals slash at one another with their teeth. The winning stag or seal will mate with many females. But fighting males seldom hurt each other badly. Instead the weaker individual gives up and creeps away.

A male animal may defend a special area called a *territory* in the breeding season. (Some animals defend territories all year round.) He may even threaten a female entering his territory, especially if she looks like a male, as female robins do. The female has to make a special "give in" sign to stop the male's attack.

Courtship

When animals have found a mate, they may behave in a special way, which helps to stop the male attacking his mate and keeps the pair together while they raise their young. For example, a male bird may bring food to a female, who pretends to be a baby bird. She crouches down, flutters her wings and lets her beak gape wide. Male and female birds may also preen the feathers of their mate.

Animal Homes and Young

Many animals do not make permanent homes. Some, such as fish, just sleep wherever they happen to be at the time. Others use natural shelters such as trees, caves or rocks. Antelope will rest under a tree, bats will roost in a cave.

However, a large number of animals build nests and shelters or dig burrows in which to sleep, hide from their enemies or raise their young. The borers and burrowers dig holes in wood, rock, sand or earth. Other creatures build complex nests of many different materials with astonishing care. Some, such as bower birds, will build huge, elaborate constructions that they add to year by year. Fish called gouramis build nests of bubbles floating on the water. Wasps make nests of paper, while ants and termites mostly work with mud. A female rabbit digs a hole and lines it with her own fur. Harvest mice weave grass stems into a hollow ball and crows build large untidy nests out of twigs.

Care of the Young

Most fish, amphibians and animals without backbones lay eggs and then leave them to chance. Such parents have to lay many eggs for very few of them survive. But certain creatures take great care of their young. They need not produce so many eggs or babies because they each have a much better chance of surviving than if they were left on their own.

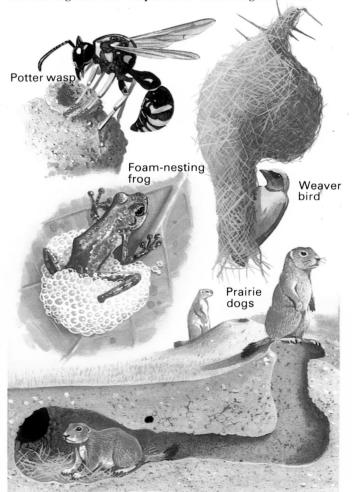

Four kinds of animal homes. The *potter wasp* molds a tiny pot-shaped nest of sand grains stuck together with saliva. She lays one egg inside. The *foam-nesting frog* lays her eggs in a ball of froth hanging from a branch. The tadpoles drop into the water below when they hatch. Young *prairie dogs* are born in the safety of underground burrows. *Weaver birds* twist strips of plant material together into complex nests which hang from trees.

Potter wasp

Foam-nesting frog

Weaver bird

Prairie dogs

Above: Baby kangaroos spend the first months of their life inside their mother's pouch. A newborn kangaroo is naked and no bigger than a person's thumb. Yet it manages to climb to the pouch where it can suckle its mother's milk in safety.

Baby animals often start life in the safety of a nest. Nests help to keep young birds and mammals warm and usually help to hide babies from enemies. Yet seabirds such as terns lay their eggs in just a small scrape in the sand of an open seashore. They breed in groups of thousands though, so parents can gang up to attack and drive away intruders.

With most birds, both parents tend the young. An ostrich cock and hen take turns to guard a nest containing many eggs laid by several ostrich hens. With many birds, though, only hens sit on the eggs. A few female insects look after their young. And female scorpions carry babies on their back. With mammals, too, mothers perform most of the work. A mother cat will lick her newborn kittens clean. A mother dolphin swims her newborn baby to the water surface for its first breath of air. All baby mammals suck milk from their mothers.

Occasionally, only fathers care for the young. The male sea horse (a small fish) guards eggs in a brood pouch in his body. A male Darwin's frog gulps up eggs laid by a female. The eggs develop into froglets in a special pouch. When they are ready, they hop out of their father's open mouth.

Some babies can fend for themselves as soon as they are born or hatch out of eggs. Newly hatched crocodiles will swim quickly away from danger. Such reptiles act largely by instinct and need little help from parents. Mammals, however, cannot look after themselves at first and some are cared for by their mothers for years.

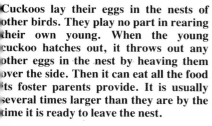

1. Female cuckoo removes some eggs already in the nest and lays her own.

2. Baby cuckoo throws out other eggs in nest.

Above: The male midwife toad wraps a string of eggs around his back legs. He carries them with him wherever he goes and dips them in water from time to time to keep them moist. After six weeks, he sits in water and waits while the tadpoles hatch and swim away.

3. Cuckoo is fed by its foster parents.

4. Young cuckoo ready to leave the nest.

Cuckoos lay their eggs in the nests of other birds. They play no part in rearing their own young. When the young cuckoo hatches out, it throws out any other eggs in the nest by heaving them over the side. Then it can eat all the food its foster parents provide. It is usually several times larger than they are by the time it is ready to leave the nest.

Right: A young chimpanzee watching its mother fishing for termites. The young chimp will soon learn to feed in the same way. Intelligent animals learn by copying their parents.

Chimpanzee

Termite mound

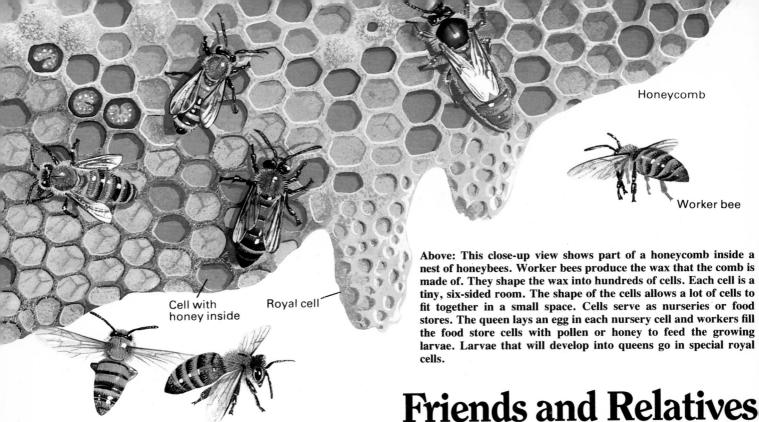

Honeycomb

Worker bee

Cell with honey inside

Royal cell

Honeybee

Above: This close-up view shows part of a honeycomb inside a nest of honeybees. Worker bees produce the wax that the comb is made of. They shape the wax into hundreds of cells. Each cell is a tiny, six-sided room. The shape of the cells allows a lot of cells to fit together in a small space. Cells serve as nurseries or food stores. The queen lays an egg in each nursery cell and workers fill the food store cells with pollen or honey to feed the growing larvae. Larvae that will develop into queens go in special royal cells.

Friends and Relatives

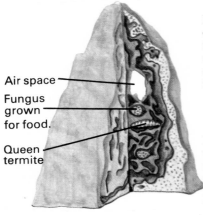

Air space

Fungus grown for food.

Queen termite

Left: A termite's nest cut open to show the structures inside. Termites are ant-like insects. They can control the temperature inside their nest.

Below: Termites built this huge nest by cementing earth together with saliva. Some termite mounds are much taller than a person.

Some animals find it more useful to live in a group rather than "going it alone." Many creatures living together find safety in numbers. There are more eyes and ears to watch out and listen for danger. An enemy that would attack a lone animal might well be confused by the sheer numbers in a moving herd of antelope, a flock of starlings or a shoal of herring. There might actually be danger for the predator too. A falcon could be injured by flying into the middle of a flock of sharp-beaked starlings, so falcons tend to leave large flocks alone.

Insect Cities

Insects such as ants, bees, wasps and termites live in insect cities. A single ant colony or beehive may be home to several thousand insects. The colony thrives because all its citizens work together although each individual has special duties to carry out.

In an ant colony, males mate with queens and queens lay eggs. Most of the eggs hatch into female workers. Small workers feed larvae that hatch out from the queen's eggs. Larger worker ants find food and bring it back to the colony. The largest workers, called soldiers, defend their colony.

Honeybees work together in a similar way. A bee that finds some food returns to the colony and performs a kind of dance. The pattern of the

Above: Apes and monkeys, such as these langurs, spend a great deal of time grooming each other. The grooming removes dry skin, dirt and parasites. This process not only keeps the animals clean but also strengthens the bonds between group members.

Above: Diagram of a troop of baboons. The adult males (green and gray) protect the females (tan) and their young (orange and blue), who stay in the center of the group. The young baboons can play there in relative safety. The troop is led by a dominant male.

Below: A crowded breeding colony of fur seals. The big bull on the right is master of this stretch of beach. The smaller seals are his females.

dance shows the direction other bees should take to reach the food. How often the bee waggles its body tells them how far away the food is.

Inside each ant colony or beehive, the ants or bees are always passing food to each other. This helps to make the insects feel they belong together. The food also tends to give all members of one colony or hive the same scent. Outsiders have other scents. This helps the guard bees and ants to recognize intruders.

Knowing Your Place

Inside a group of mammals such as apes or monkeys, individuals give each other food or help to clean each other. This give-and-take helps to keep the members of a group together. But they are not all equal. Some hold a higher rank than others – this is called a *pecking order*. Chickens have a pecking order as well and this is where the name came from. The most aggressive individual holds the highest rank. This animal will nip or peck any of the rest and none of them fight back. The animal holding the second highest rank nips or pecks all but the top ranking animal. And so on down the pecking order.

But rank is not always fixed. A female monkey and her offspring take the rank of the male she mates with. Any individuals that fall ill may drop several places in the pecking order.

The Changing Seasons

In some parts of the world, each year consists of four seasons – spring, summer, autumn and winter. Plants and animals make the most of the warmer seasons and manage to survive the colder ones in a variety of ways.

In spring, new leaves grow from the bare branches of trees such as oaks and beeches. Seeds sprout, insects hatch and birds build nests and lay their eggs. Mammals such as rabbits, mice and foxes have their babies. These young animals start life when food is just becoming plentiful.

In summer, plants grow thick and fast and many produce flowers. Insects visit the flowers to feed on pollen and nectar. Young mice and rabbits munch tender grasses while foxes and owls catch some of the mice and rabbits to feed to their own young.

Autumn brings many changes. Many plants produce seeds and some trees lose their leaves. Mammals such as bears and hedgehogs try to eat enough food to last them through the winter. Lizards, snakes and frogs hide underground as the days grow chilly.

In winter, the days are short and cold. Frost kills many soft-stemmed plants and insects that cannot hide away from the cold. Hedgehogs and bears sleep through the winter but rabbits, weasels and foxes stay awake and have to search for food.

Right: In autumn, the leaves of deciduous trees turn yellow, red and orange and begin to fall off the trees. This helps the trees to survive the winter by reducing water loss.
Below: The short-tailed weasel in its winter coat. In northern lands, weasels and stoats turn white in winter. Because they match the snow around them, their enemies cannot see them easily.

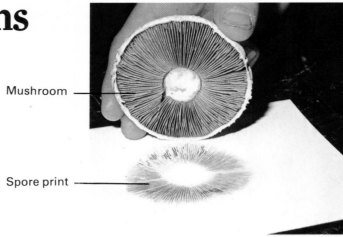

Mushroom

Spore print

Above: Fungi usually produce fruiting bodies, such as mushrooms and toadstools, in late summer or autumn. These fruiting bodies give off many thousands of spores, which can grow into new fungi. Try leaving a mushroom on a piece of paper overnight. The spores that fall off make a ray-like pattern.

Amazing Journeys

Certain birds, mammals and other animals are tremendous travelers. Each year they journey many hundreds or even thousands of miles, often going without food or water for several days. This is called *migration*. Animals migrate mostly to escape the cold or find new feeding grounds. Each spring, some warblers, ducks, geese, swans and wading birds fly north. They raise their young in the long, warm summer days of northern lands when food is plentiful. In autumn, when food becomes scarce, the temperature drops and the days grow shorter, the migrants and their young fly south to a warmer climate.

Birds are not the only airborne migrants. Bats fly long distances overland as well. Some butterflies can also travel long distances. Monarch butterflies that breed in Canada fly south for the winter and millions of these creatures spend the winter clustered on tall trees in Mexico. Deer called caribou spend summer grazing in Arctic North America. As summer fades, they trek far south to sheltered forests. In spring they wander north again, feeding on the fresh green shoots that sprout.

Migrations go on even in the sea. Some sea turtles will swim half way across the Atlantic ocean from Brazil to lay their eggs on Ascension island in the South Atlantic. Gray whales feed in Arctic waters but swim south all the way to Mexico to breed. No other mammals in the world regularly travel so far.

Above and left: The red arrows on these maps show the migration routes of the arctic tern (above) and the monarch butterfly (left).

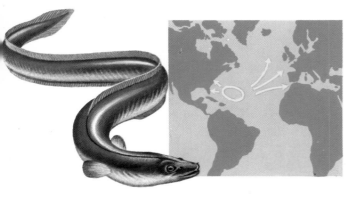

Above: Once in their lifetime, adult eels cross the Atlantic Ocean. They spawn in the Sargasso Sea – the ringed area of the map. Then they die. But ocean currents take their young back across the ocean to the United States or Europe.

Below: Some caribou migrate south for up to 800 miles (1300 kilometers) each autumn. Next spring they return north.

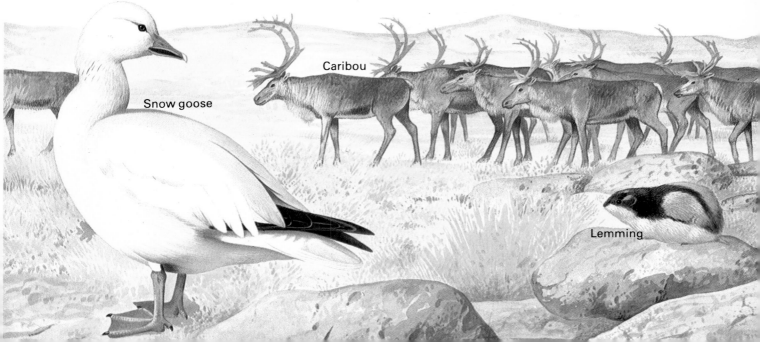

Snow goose

Caribou

Lemming

Desert Survival

Desert plants and animals manage to survive in the driest lands on earth. Many also manage to endure tremendous heat.

Some desert plants produce long roots that suck up moisture from deep down, while other plants have shorter roots that stretch over a wider area to catch the rain that occasionally soaks the surface of the ground. Most long-lived desert plants store water in juicy tubers, bulbs or stems. Cacti have waxy stems to stop water leaking out and some also have pleated stems that expand like an accordion to take up as much water as possible when it does rain. Many desert plants survive as seeds buried in the sand. As soon as there is any rain, they suddenly sprout and produce flowers and seeds.

Animals cope with the heat and drought in various ways. Some lizards feed in the cool of the mornings and evenings and burrow into the sand to escape the midday heat. Reptiles that move around at midday are able to avoid being burned by the desert surface. One lizard lifts each foot off the ground in turn and another rears on its back legs to stay in the shade behind a narrow plant.

Desert animals obtain moisture by eating juicy plants or other animals. Most creatures need to eat each day but camels can survive for days without food or drink. They store food as fat inside their humps. Camels do not sweat until their body temperature rises very high indeed. In this way they lose little moisture from their bodies.

Above: The narras melon from southern Africa sucks up water with roots that grow far longer than its stems. The roots can grow up to 40 feet (12 meters) in their search for moisture.
Below: The desert cricket supports its weight on feet like tiny branches, which give it a good grip on the loose sand. This also keeps most of the cricket's body away from the hot desert surface.

Right: The body of a sidewinder snake hardly touches the ground as it throws itself across the hot desert sand.
Below: A barrel cactus swells up after rain as its pleats fill up with moisture. But after months of drought, its pleats have lost much of their stored water, so the plant looks thinner.

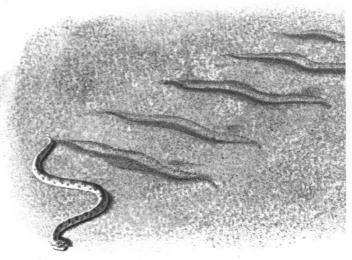

Life at the Top

The upper slopes of high mountains are cold, dry and windy. The air is thin and the soil is poor. High mountains are among the harshest places anywhere on earth.

Although the cold wind kills off most trees, other plants survive. Many form low clumps that hug the ground to avoid the wind, while some have hairy leaves that help to trap warmth and moisture. Africa's giant lobelias rise high above the ground, but a thick, corky stem and clusters of dead leaves protect their living tissues from the intense cold.

Birds and mammals also manage to survive among the mountain peaks. Crows and eagles soar high on rising air currents. Mountain goats and sheep leap nimbly from rock to rock. Their springy limbs are tipped with hooves that are specially adapted to cope with slippery rock surfaces. A hollow below each hoof allows it to grip the rock like a suction pad and a small "claw" behind the hoof gives extra balance. Thick coats help to keep these large mammals warm but many move downhill to find food when snow buries the plants.

Small mountain mammals burrow to escape the winter cold. In winter, pikas feed on heaps of hay they have collected and stored. One species of pika lives on Mount Everest at heights of up to 18,000 feet. These little relatives of rabbits stay active all year round but other rodents, such as alpine marmots, hibernate. They spend nearly half the year sleeping.

Above: Flowers of the purple saxifrage, which grows as a low cushion and clings closely to the mountain soil. The low creeping stems and small leaves help to prevent loss of water in the windswept places in which it grows. Larger plants would be blown over by the wind or lose all their water by evaporation in the strong winds high on mountains.

Left: An ibex perches on a rocky crag in the mountains. Among the steep cliffs, this mountaineer is safe from almost all enemies but human hunters. Seven species of wild goat are called ibex. They live in the rugged mountains of Africa and Eurasia. Their hoofs have sharp edges, which dig into rock crevices as they climb. They also have hollow soles to their feet, which grip the rocks like suction pads. This allows them to leap up incredibly steep rock faces.

On the Grasslands

Large parts of the world look like seas of grass. Grasses grow in lands too dry for large areas of trees.

Tropical Grasslands

Tall grasses and scattered trees cover the world's hot dry grasslands, which are called *savannas*. Africa's savannas are home to large grazing mammals, such as antelope and zebra. Huge herds crop the grass as they wander over the plains. Even though the animals eat the tops of the grass, it goes on growing from the base, so grazing does not kill it.

A variety of different animals can live side by side because they each need a slightly different kind of food. For instance, zebras munch long, tough grasses, gazelles graze on young grass shoots, antelopes called lesser kudus browse on bushes and giraffes eat leaves growing high on the scattered trees. Grazers also give the grass a rest by moving on from time to time. In Southern Tanzania elephants, buffaloes and hippopotamuses all eat and trample tall marsh grass at the end of the rainy season. Then they move away to find fresh feeding grounds. This gives the marsh grass time to grow new, tender shoots. These shoots in turn attract such grazing antelopes as hartebeest and eland.

Fierce carnivores such as lions and cheetahs attack the large savanna grazers. Cheetahs can outsprint the fastest antelope unless it twists and turns, and packs of hyenas and hunting dogs can run down and kill animals as large as wildebeest and zebra. Leopards usually hunt alone. They often prefer to lie on a branch overhanging a path and pounce on creatures passing underneath. After the carnivores have eaten, scavengers move in to share the feast. Jackals, vultures and marabou storks gobble up whatever lions, leopards and hyenas leave.

Prairies and Steppes

The North American grasslands and Asian steppes are called *temperate grasslands*. Here the grass is shorter then on the African savanna and there are fewer trees. Huge herds of large grazing animals, such as bison and wild horses, once lived here but most have been killed off by human hunters.

The most common steppe and prairie animals today are smaller creatures such as birds and rodents, which feed off the grasses or seeds of flowering plants. In North America, large plump rodents known as prairie dogs dig burrows that form underground "towns." Burrowing owls and rattlesnakes move in to share these homes. The owls kill and eat prairie dogs while the snakes eat the prairie dogs and the owls' eggs.

Below: African grazing and browsing animals at a savanna waterhole. A lot of different grazing animals can survive together because they feed on different sorts of grasses and leaves.

Below: Lions gnaw the flesh from the carcass of a grazing animal that they have killed. Lionesses work together to stalk and tackle their prey.

In the Forests

Forests and woods can be found in many parts of the world and in many different climates. Some trees can exist in extreme cold, whereas others thrive in an atmosphere which is rather like a hot, steamy bathroom. The plants or animals of any forest depend on where the forest is. Tropical forests, temperate forests and cold forests each have their special type of wildlife.

The largest area of forest is in the northern hemisphere and stretches from North America, across Northern Europe to Asia. The trees here are mostly evergreen conifers with needle-like leaves, which do not lose their moisture in winter. Plant-eaters here include squirrels and deer while lynx, wolves and bears are among the largest predators.

South of the conifer belt, are patches of broadleaved woodland where deciduous trees such as oaks and beeches thrive. These trees lose their leaves in autumn. The fallen leaves form a rich carpet of compost – food for many small insects and nourishment for an undergrowth of bushes and flowering plants.

Close to the equator, tropical rainforests grow in a climate that is hot and rainy. There are no extremes of temperature, so most of the trees are evergreen and broad-leaved. There is a huge variety of trees in these forests. A European woodland may have 12 kinds of trees, whereas hundreds of different kinds grow in a tropical forest, supporting a large animal population in all its different levels.

The forest floor is home to plant-eaters such as rodents, forest antelopes and Indian elephants. But most creatures live high among the trees. Apes and monkeys swing through the branches, parrots and toucans feed on treetop fruits, butterflies flit among the treetop flowers and frogs and snakes hide among the leaves.

Below: These four pictures show four stages in the growth of a red deer's antlers.

1. Knobs grow on bones on top of head.

2. Antlers covered in a soft skin called *velvet*.

3. Blood vessels under velvet carry food and minerals to growing antlers.

4. Blood supply to antlers is cut off and velvet is rubbed off before breeding season.

Below: The layers of plants in a tropical rain forest. The taller trees shut out much of the light from the forest floor but ferns and mosses thrive in the damp gloom.

Below: Woodpeckers chisel into decaying tree trunks to search for insects and other small animals. They have a long, sticky tongue to lick up insects.

A Watery Home

Each quiet pool or bubbling river is home to a variety of plants and animals. Different parts of a pond or river attract different forms of plant life. Marsh marigolds and reeds sprout from the muddy rims of shallow ponds and marshes. In deeper water, the long stems of water lilies lift their leaves to the surface. The richest part of a pond or river is around the edge where most of the plants grow. Here countless tiny crustaceans, insect larvae, mollusks and worms live and feed off the plants. These animals form food for newts and many water insects.

Further out in the water, water snails, tadpoles and some fish graze on mossy algae growing on underwater plants and stones. Fierce hunters such as dragonfly larvae, water beetles and fisher spiders seize tadpoles and small fish such as sticklebacks. Caddis fly larvae may escape unseen. These insects hide their bodies with a covering of sand grains, tiny stones or bits of plants. And few animals could catch the agile pond skaters as they skim across the surface of the water on their long legs. Trout and perch prowl on the watch for fish smaller than themselves. Large pike will snap up trout and

Above: The North American fisher spider climbs down water plants to feed but must come to the surface to breathe.

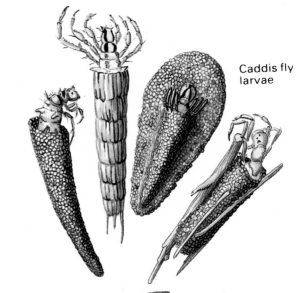

Caddis fly larvae

Right: The larvae of most kinds of caddis fly make tube-like homes for themselves out of small stones, pieces of water plants and other debris. Each species makes its home in a particular pattern. They usually carry their homes around with them, which helps to protect them from enemies. Adult caddis flies are moth-like insects with long wings covered in hairs.
Below: A remarkable variety of freshwater fish live in tropical pools or streams. The piranha fish of South America has razor-sharp teeth. A shoal of these fish can reduce a horse to a skeleton within minutes.

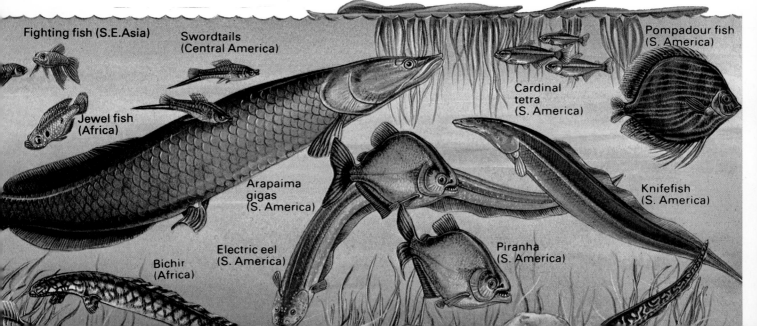

Fighting fish (S.E.Asia)
Swordtails (Central America)
Pompadour fish (S. America)
Cardinal tetra (S. America)
Jewel fish (Africa)
Arapaima gigas (S. America)
Knifefish (S. America)
Electric eel (S. America)
Bichir (Africa)
Piranha (S. America)

Above: The nautilus is a relative of the octopus. It swims one way by squirting out water in the opposite direction.

Bottle-nosed
dolphin

perch. Between them, herons, otters, mink and bears can tackle fish of almost any size.

In the sea, as in fresh water or on land, plants are eaten by small animals which in turn are eaten by larger ones. A drop of sea water teems with thousands of tiny drifting plants and animals called *plankton*. The plants are known as *phytoplankton*. Feeding on them are animals called *zooplankton*. These may include young jelly fishes, crabs, sea worms and other animals without backbones. All these form food for small fishes hunting near the surface of the sea. Even the world's largest whales feed on little shrimp-like creatures called krill.

Small fish in their turn fall prey to larger ones. Millions of sardines and anchovies are gobbled up by predators such as mackerel, which are themselves eaten by sharks and tunas. Killer whales eat fish but will also tackle whales far larger than themselves. Whales and seals are mammals. They can swim as well as fish but they have to come to the surface to breathe. Some species can remain underwater for more than an hour.

Way down in the ocean depths live strange sea creatures that never see daylight. These fish feed on one another and on dead and dying animals that drift down from the sunlit surface. Most deep-sea fish have huge jaws to snap up any food that comes their way.

Left: The bottle-nosed dolphin is a mammal (like you) and breathes air through a blowhole on the top of its head. It has a smooth, streamlined body, which helps it to swim fast through the water. It moves its strong tail up and down to push it along. (Fish move their tails from side to side.)
Below: Some of the animals that live on a coral reef, which is built up from the skeletons of tiny animals related to the sea anemones. Most coral reefs grow in warm, clear, sunlit tropical seas.

Giant clam

Rainbow parrot fish

Zebra
angel fish

Corals

Soldier
fish

Protecting Nature

Wild plants and animals are in danger almost everywhere and people are one of their greatest enemies. For instance, hunters have killed so many whales and rhinoceroses that some species could vanish forever. Collectors have dug up so many venus fly traps that these insect-eating plants have become quite rare.

Poisons and Pollution

Many harmless creatures have suffered from the chemical poisons (*pesticides*) sprayed on insect pests. Spilt chemicals are another threat to wildlife. When an oil tanker is wrecked, huge amounts of oil may leak into the sea. The oil destroys the waterproofing on the feathers of seabirds so that they drown. They may also die from swallowing the oil as they try to use their beaks to clean up their feathers. Untreated sewage and industrial wastes poured into rivers reduce the oxygen content of the water and poison it so it is unfit for fish and other water creatures.

Above: People and machines clearing tropical rainforest in South America to make way for a new road. Tropical rainforests are probably the richest habitats in the world. If forest creatures cannot find new homes, they will die.

Above: The lady's slipper orchid is a rare plant. Some of the places where orchids grow have to be guarded by conservationists to stop orchid collectors digging up the plants.

Left: The giant panda is a rare animal that lives on remote mountainsides in southwestern China. It may be in danger of extinction if the bamboo forests it lives in are destroyed.

Below: A plane spraying insecticide. Pesticide that kills insects may collect in the bodies of insect-eating animals. Birds that eat the poisoned animals might die.

Destroying Wild Places

The greatest threat to wildlife is probably the disappearance of wild places. Each year, timber workers around the world chop down forests equal to the size of Indiana, engineers drain marshes, builders cover heaths and fields with roads and cities and farmers dig up hedges. Such destruction could kill off a million kinds of plants and animals before the year 2000.

Saving Wildlife

Luckily much is being done to save the world's endangered wildlife. Some governments forbid hunters to kill rare animals such as the white rhinoceros or the blue whale. A ban on hunting blue whales may have come just in time to save the largest animals that have ever lived on the earth. Some governments also forbid traders to buy or sell rare animals. If collectors cannot sell the wild animals they catch, they tend to leave those animals alone.

Chemists have discovered safer pesticides than those used in the 1950s. Scientists can also now produce chemicals that kill specific plant or animal pests without harming other wildlife. Some of the chemicals they use are made by plants or animals themselves.

Oil companies, factories and cities can do much to prevent poisons leaking into seas or rivers. For example, sewage treatment has helped to clean up Lake Erie, making it a safe home for fish and wildlife for the first time in many years. But sewage and factory wastes will continue to poison rivers in countries too poor to pay for cleaning up their waterways.

Many nations have set aside national parks and nature reserves as safe homes for wild plants and animals. Game wardens work to keep out poachers. But even nature reserves may not save the rarest creatures. Instead biologists try to breed them in special zoos or parks. This sort of process has saved the Hawaiian né-né goose and the graceful Arabian oryx. For many other endangered species captive breeding may be their only hope of survival.

Right: A conservation group at work in a British woodland. They are clearing scrub and coppicing some of the smaller trees. Coppicing involves cutting the trees down to a stump to encourage many thin shoots to grow. This lets light into the wood and allows flowers and shrubs to grow beneath the trees, providing homes for wildlife.

Above: A boat belonging to the Greenpeace conservation group, which tries to prevent people catching whales or dumping poisonous wastes at sea. Group members go out from the large ship in small boats and try to make it impossible for the killing or dumping to take place.

Above: A scientist removing wading birds from a trap on the coast of the Camargue, in southern France. The birds are ringed and measured and the details recorded. Scientists have to learn as much as possible about plants and animals so that they can plan to conserve them.

In 1650 Archbishop Ussher calculated that the earth was created on October 2, 4004 BC at 9 o'clock in the morning. He worked this out by adding up the generations listed in the Bible.

Left: This fossil *trilobite* is about 390 million years old. It would have looked frightening to people in the 17th century before the true nature of fossils was understood.

Right: A fossil sea urchin called *Hemicidaris* with its spines well preserved. These sea urchins lived in Jurassic and Cretaceous times – from 190 to 65 million years ago.

Evolution — the History of an Idea

The idea that living things have changed during the history of life on earth is more than two thousand years old. In Roman times, the philosopher and poet *Lucretius* reviewed this subject in his book on human knowledge. But the religious dominance in Europe during the next 16 centuries ensured that the explanation of the Bible, in the book of Genesis, was accepted with few questions.

In the 17th and 18th centuries, explorers began to bring back many new plants and animals to Europe from far-off lands. And naturalists, such as John Ray and Carolus Linnaeus, were discovering order in the complex variety of plants and animals. They found that all plants and animals could be arranged in groups (*classified*) according to the features they had in common. Fossils and the huge bones of prehistoric animals were also being discovered. But most people of the time grasped at a religious explanation for these discoveries. The fossils and bones were thought to be the remains of animals that had perished in the great flood described in the Bible.

However, the naturalists and the men who were beginning to study the rocks of the earth (the geologists) found that certain kinds of fossils were found in certain rocks. They also discovered that layer upon layer of rocks had been formed in past ages. This led to the idea that the earth and the life it supported might be very ancient indeed – much older than the date of 4004 B.C. worked out by Archbishop Ussher in the mid-17th century from writings in the Bible. Thinking men began to ask questions and look at living things and the rocks and fossils of the earth for answers, rather than accepting the traditional doctrines developed two thousand years previously.

Erasmus Darwin, the physician grandfather of Charles Darwin, suggested two hundred years ago that living things might acquire "new powers and larger limbs" because of their needs and actions. At about the same time, the French naturalist George Buffon, wrote a monumental series of books on natural history in which he maintained that living things have changed and advanced during the history of life on earth. But neither of these two scholars (nor anyone else) could explain how these changes came about.

Jean Baptiste Lamarck (1744-1829) This French naturalist was one of the first to suggest a way in which evolution might work. He suggested that characteristics which plants and animals gained in their own lifetime could be passed on to their offspring. Discoveries in genetics have shown his ideas to be wrong.

Alfred Russel Wallace (1823-1913) An English naturalist who worked in the jungles of Indonesia and came up with the same explanation as Charles Darwin for how evolution might work. In 1857 Wallace wrote to Darwin outlining his ideas and this forced Darwin to publish.

Charles Darwin (1809-1882)
This painting shows Darwin in 1840, four years after he returned from his famous voyage on H.M.S. *Beagle*.

The First Theories of Evolution

In 1809, the great French biologist Jean Baptiste Lamarck published his "Zoological Philosophy," which included his theory of evolution. He believed that animals and plants could acquire new characteristics during their own lifetimes in order to cope with their environment. For example, giraffes had evolved long necks because generations of giraffes stretched their necks to reach the juicy young leaves high up in trees. This seemed a very reasonable theory and many people accepted it at the time, although Lamarck was later shown to be wrong. However, he did give an essential lead to the man who was the first to explain how evolution could have taken place. This man was Charles Darwin.

As a young man, Darwin spent five years sailing around the world as a naturalist on H.M.S. *Beagle*. His discoveries and observations during the voyage helped him to think of a scientific explanation for how evolution might have happened, but he did not publish his theory immediately. He worked quietly at his home in Kent, England, for the next twenty years, carefully gathering evidence to support his theory. Then one day, a letter arrived from a fellow biologist, Alfred Wallace, who was collecting animals and plants in the tropics. The letter was a dreadful shock to Darwin. Quite

independently, Wallace had come up with the same theory of how evolution might work.

To solve the difficulty, the ideas of the two biologists were read out at the same time at a meeting of the Linnaean Society in London in 1858. The following year Darwin published his book *The Origin of Species*, which contained a detailed explanation of his theory.

Briefly, the theory that Darwin and Wallace offered went like this: All species produce far more offspring than can possibly survive to reproduce. Their numbers are controlled by factors in the environment, such as food supply, living space and links with other species. But which individuals are most likely to survive?

No two living things are exactly alike and the individuals with the best chance of surviving will be those best suited to their particular environment and way of life. They will pass on their characteristics (which are controlled by their genetic instructions) to the next generations (see pages 114-119). If the environment changes, those animals and plants best suited to the new environment are most likely to survive and reproduce. Over very long periods of time, one species could change into another.

Darwin called his idea *natural selection* and believed it explained how the enormous diversity of life on earth had evolved. Darwin's ideas still form the basis of evolutionary biology.

Evidence for Evolution

The scientific theory of evolution suggests a slow process that takes place over millions of years. It is therefore not possible to watch one species changing into another. Most of the evidence supporting the theory of evolution has been collected since Darwin's time. It comes from the appearance, internal structure, biochemistry and behavior of living species as well as the relationships between living species and their fossil relatives. You can find out more on the next six pages.

The Case of the Speckled Moths

The best known example of natural selection in action is that of the speckled moths. These moths are fairly common in Britain. They are eaten by several species of birds, which take them from the tree trunks where they rest during the day.

In the early 19th century (before the industrial revolution) most of the moths were whitish. They blended well with the pale-colored lichens on the tree trunks, so birds found them difficult to spot. A lot of whitish moths survived to reproduce and pass on their genes.

But by the end of the 19th century, pollution from factories had killed off most of the lichens and blackened the tree trunks in industrial areas. The blackish moths (which were present in small numbers in the original population)

Above: Observations of living species can provide clues to how species might have formed in the past. These four species of Hawaiian honeycreeper do not compete with each other because their beaks are adapted to different diets. They probably evolved from a finch-like ancestor that reached Hawaii from the North American mainland. Eventually they became so different they could no longer interbreed and were different species.

matched the blackened tree trunks and were more likely to survive attacks by birds. So the numbers of blackish moths gradually built up. The characteristics of the population changed to survive the change in the environment. Today, however, since the environment has been cleaned up and the trees are less polluted, the whitish moth is replacing the blackish form again.

Natural changes to the environment are not usually as rapid or clear-cut as changes caused by people. So it is often difficult for scientists to work out how the environment might be affecting the evolution of a population in nature.

Left: Two speckled moths on a tree trunk. Which one is most likely to be eaten by a bird?
Below and right: Three of the many breeds of dog that have been developed from the wolf over many thousands of years. This shows how the characteristics of a species can be changed by selecting which individuals breed together.
Top right: Tibetan spaniel.
Bottom left: Scottish terrier.
Bottom right: Saluki.

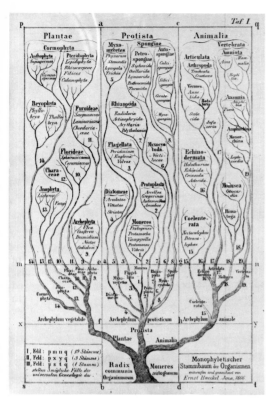

Above: Part of a "family tree" drawn by the German biologist Ernst Haeckel in 1866 to show how various animal groups could be related by evolution.

Below: Animals often have similar features, which suggests they may have evolved from the same ancestor. The front limbs of these vertebrates are all made of the same bones (with five digits at the end) arranged in different ways. Each limb is adapted for a different way of life. But sometimes animals may have similar structures because they live in the same environment, not because they are related. For example, dolphins and fish look alike because they are both adapted for swimming fast in the sea. But they are not related. Dolphins are mammals.

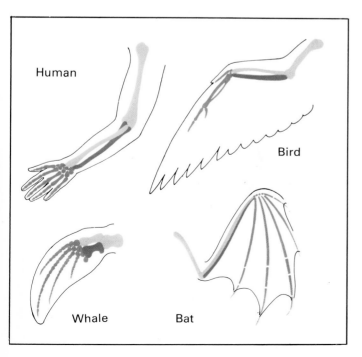

Tracing Family Trees

Biologists sort living things and fossils into groups (classify them) based on certain features they share in common. The similarities between some groups suggest they may have evolved from the same ancestor. Some modern systems of classification suggest relationships between living and fossil plants and animals, which shows how they might have evolved.

From Chaos to Order

Until the middle of the 18th century, naturalists classified plants and animals in different ways. There was no standard way of describing or naming each kind of organism. So when naturalists talked about their discoveries it was often difficult to know precisely which plant or animal they were referring to. The situation was chaotic and unscientific.

An Englishman named John Ray was the first person to arrange plants and animals in a more scientific way. He realized that a system of classification had to be based on the structure of organisms, not the kind of food they ate or the climate they lived in. Carolus Linnaeus carried forward Ray's basic ideas. In 1753 he established the system of naming and classifying living things that is used everywhere today.

The science of classification is called *taxonomy*. Organisms are first split into *kingdoms* (such as the animal and plant kingdoms), which are then divided into smaller groups called *phyla* (singular phylum). The members of each phylum have certain features in common which separate them from members of other phyla. Each phylum is broken down into *classes*, classes are divided into *orders*, orders into *families*, families into *genera* (singular genus) and genera into *species*.

A species is a group of plants or animals whose members have most features in common. They usually look and behave alike and can breed among themselves. (It is not always possible to find out about breeding behavior, so biologists sometimes have to base their classifications on just physical features.) Each species has two names. The first one is the name of the genus to which the species belongs and the second is a special name used only for that species. For example, the rabbit, *Lepus cuniculus*, and the hare *Lepus timidus*, are two species in the genus *Lepus*.

HOW FOSSILS ARE FORMED

Above: The footprint of a dinosaur called *Cheirotherium*, which walked over a patch of mud about 150 million years ago. The mud hardened and was later covered by sediment, which preserved the footprint.

Below: This fossil of a seed fern *Neuropteris* is made of a thin film of carbon.

1. An ammonite died and was buried on the seabed.

2. It was dissolved away to form a fossil mould.

3. The mold was filled by sediment to form a fossil cast.

The diagrams above show how a fossil mold or cast may form.

Above: The sticky resin from a conifer tree has hardened into amber to preserve this ancient insect.

Below: These stone "tree trunks" are in Petrified Forest National Park in Eastern Arizona. (*Petrified* means "turned to stone.") They were formed when minerals dissolved in water seeped inside the wood and replaced the internal structure of the tree.

Fossils — the Key to the Past

The collection and study of *fossils* (the preserved remains of plants or animals) has enabled biologists to piece together the history of life on earth. Fossils provide the most direct evidence for evolution, although there are many gaps in the story they reveal. This is mainly because only a very small fraction of the plants and animals from the past are likely to have been preserved as fossils, although many fossils have yet to be discovered.

Where are Fossils Formed?

Plants and animals have to be buried quickly to stand a good chance of becoming a fossil. The most likely place for quick burial is in the sea where mud and sand washed off the land collects in layers called *sediments*. This explains why many fossils are of sea creatures, such as shellfish, sea urchins and corals. Most parts of the earth's surface have been covered by sea at some time in the earth's history and rocks that were once at the bottom of the sea have been pushed up into mountain ranges. So fossils of sea creatures can be collected in most places on dry land.

Fossils can also form on land in lakes, ponds, natural tar pits and frozen earth. Mammoths preserved in the frozen soil of the Arctic for 45,000 years still had a covering of hair and skin, and food in their stomachs.

1 When an animal, such as this dinosaur, dies, its body may be buried quickly underwater.

2 The body will decay but the bones may be replaced by minerals to form a stone fossil. This may be pushed to the surface by earth movements and uncovered later.

How Fossils are Formed

Most fossils are formed when the hard parts of a plant or animal are dissolved away and replaced by minerals from the sediment they are buried in. This eventually forms a stone copy of the original organism. In some fossils, the hard parts are replaced so slowly that the finest details of the original may be preserved. It can take tens of millions of years for the process of fossilization to be completed.

Shells may be buried and dissolved away so that a hollow space or *mold* remains after the shell has disappeared. If the space is filled with mineral material, a *cast* of the original shell is formed.

Other Kinds of Fossils

Stone copies, molds or casts are not the only sorts of fossils. The buried remains of plants are sometimes converted to thin films of carbon, which are preserved sandwiched between the layers of a rock. The soft parts of an animal, such as its skin, may occasionally form fossils. Impressions also exist of whole organisms, such as jellyfish or starfish. Whole insects have been preserved when they were trapped in the resin oozing from trees. The resin later hardened to form *amber*.

Sometimes the animals themselves are not preserved but their tracks are. These are called *trace fossils* and include the footprints made by our ancestors one million years ago in Africa.

Dating Past Life

Fossils are formed from stone so they are associated with rocks. And because some rocks and fossils contain radioactive forms of elements (such as uranium and potassium) they can be dated. The basic principle behind *radioactive dating* is that each radioactive element decays at a known rate. The decay rates of elements used to date most fossils vary from several hundred million years to several billion years. So a radioactive element is like a clock ticking away.

Scientists must find out two things before a date can be worked out – the proportion of the element that would have been in the rock or fossil when it formed and the proportion remaining today. From this, scientists can calculate the age of rocks and fossils.

C14 Dating

With less ancient specimens, the actual remains of animals and plants can be dated. All living things contain a certain amount of radioactive carbon (carbon 14). This carbon is being formed all the time by high energy cosmic rays which penetrate the earth's atmosphere. When an organism dies, it cannot take any more carbon 14 into its body tissues. The carbon 14 then begins to decay at a known rate. So by testing a specimen to find out how much carbon 14 it contains, scientists can calculate its age. However, this technique can only be used if the specimen is less than about 50,000 years old.

Below left: A scientist uncovering a fossil *Tarbosaurus*, a huge flesh-eating dinosaur that lived more than 65 million years ago.
Below right: The age of plant and animal remains up to about 50,000 years old can be calculated from the radioactive carbon they contain. Older fossils are less radioactive.

5600 yrs old

11,200 yrs old

44,000 yrs old

The Fossil Record and Catastrophes

Many scientists believe that the direction of evolution has been changed by physical catastrophes that have dramatically affected conditions on earth. Biologists and geologists have found evidence of several such catastrophes in the long history of our planet.

Enormous meteorites, perhaps six miles (ten kilometers) across have struck the earth in prehistoric times. Geological survey satellites can photograph the distinct outlines of huge craters, which are not easily detectable at ground level. There is some evidence that the dinosaurs may have become extinct because of changes to the earth's climate caused by a giant meteorite striking the earth. The birds and mammals evolved in a spectacular way after the dinosaurs became extinct.

The ammonites, a great dynasty of sea creatures, existed for 330 million years. But they became extinct at about the same time as the dinosaurs.

Doctors David Raup and John Sepkoski of the University of Chicago have claimed that mass extinctions have taken place at regular intervals of 26 million years during the history of the earth. Such regular occurrences would be likely to have an astronomical cause. Many scientists do not accept all the claims by the Chicago scientists, but they do believe that random events, sometimes very dramatic ones, have changed environments on earth so much that life on this planet has been remodeled from time to time. And scientists agree that environments change (even if this takes place slowly over millions of years) and species change as they adapt to new environments.

Below: If an environment does not change, its animals and plants may not change. Many species of lobe-finned fishes existed about 350 million years ago. Today a fish called the *Coelacanth* is the last surviving member of this group (as far as we know). It may have survived because it lives in an unchanging, deep sea environment to which it is well adapted.

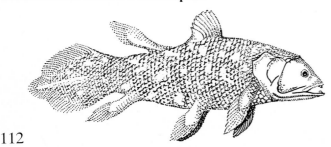

THE SCALE OF LIFE

The time scale of life on earth is often difficult to understand. In the diagram to the right, the whole history of life has been condensed into one year. Man appeared late in the evening of December 31st and one human lifetime lasts just one second.

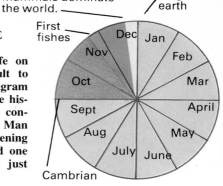

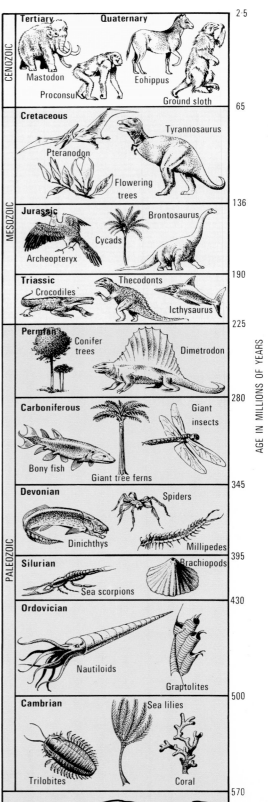

Below: Scientists have collected evidence to show that the continents slowly move about the earth's surface like huge rafts. This idea is called *continental drift*. Evidence shows that the continents were once joined together in a huge supercontinent called *Pangaea*. This continent began to break up some 200 million years ago and its parts (today's continents) moved slowly away from each other. Fossils of the plant *Glossopteris* and land animals such as *Mesosaurus* and *Lystrosaurus* have been found on continents that are now widely separated. The position of the continents affects the climate and this has probably affected the course of evolution over a long period of time.

Below: The map below shows the maximum extent of the ice in the Pleistocene Ice Ages, which took place in the northern hemisphere between 1.8 million and 10,000 years ago. This affected the climate worldwide and caused evolutionary changes. Many animals and plants became extinct. Some moved south to warmer climates and those that remained adapted to survive the new conditions. Many of the animals, such as the woolly mammoth and the woolly rhinoceros, evolved warm coats. They lived around the edge of the ice sheets. But many of these animals appear to have died out because they were hunted by man.

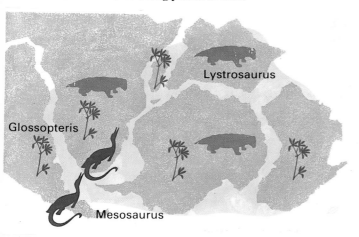

Lystrosaurus

Glossopteris

Mesosaurus

Below: Dinosaurs ruled the earth for about 140 million years but they had all died out by about 65 million years ago. The reason for their extinction is one of the great puzzles of the past, although many theories have been suggested. One of the most likely explanations is a sweeping change in climate, caused perhaps by continental drift and earth movements, which cooled the earth. Other theories involve meteorites or comets from space causing a change in climate, or natural disasters, such as floods. Some scientists have suggested the dinosaurs may have been the victims of disease or plant poisons but these ideas do not explain why a variety of animals unrelated to the dinosaurs died out at the same time. Another theory is that small mammals ate the dinosaur eggs and helped to bring about their downfall. Which explanation do you think is most likely?

The flesh-eating mammal-like reptile *Lycaenops* attacking a plant-eating dicynodont. These dinosaurs lived in Permian times – about 250 million years ago.

Mendel and the Laws of Heredity

In any species, be it beetles or buttercups, there are variations in the features of the individual animals or plants. The theory of evolution states that those individuals with features best suited to their environment and way of life are more likely to survive. They are likely to produce more offspring than other individuals. Darwin and Wallace (see page 107) realized that plants and animals must be able to pass on their favorable characteristics to their offspring and that in this way species changed (evolved) over many generations. But they knew nothing about how this process, which is called *inheritance* or *heredity*, works.

In 1866, only seven years after Darwin had published the *Origin of Species*, an Austrian monk, Gregor Mendel, published a scientific paper explaining the laws of heredity. But Mendel's work was ignored until three scientists rediscovered his results at the beginning of the 20th century.

Mendel's Experiments

Mendel's research was carried out with garden peas and other plants in his monastery garden in Brunn, Austria (now Brno in Czechoslovakia). Peas were a particularly good experimental plant because they had characteristics (such as short or tall stems and smooth or wrinkled seeds), which could be easily observed and counted in experiments. Mendel transferred pollen by hand from the male to the female parts of his experimental flowers to produce seeds and carefully recorded the results. For example, he used the pollen from tall-stemmed plants to fertilize short-stemmed plants. All the offspring grown from the seeds had tall stems. (This went against the popular belief of the time, which was that the characteristics of the parents would somehow be blended together in the offspring to produce plants of medium height.)

But what had happened to the short-stemmed characteristic? Had it been lost? Mendel continued his experiment and went on to breed the tall-stemmed plants he had produced with each other. And he found that one in four of the

Above: Although the members of a family have many of the same features, each individual (except for identical twins) is slightly different. Without this variation, evolution could not take place.

Below: These diagrams show one of the experiments that helped Mendel to work out his laws of heredity. In the first diagram, you can see what happens when a tall and a short plant are cross-fertilized. Each parent plant has two genes for height but it passes on only one of these genes to each of its offspring.

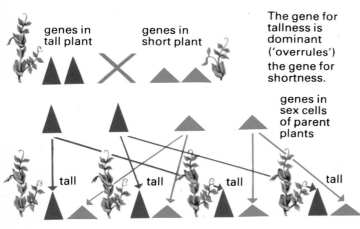

genes in tall plant genes in short plant

The gene for tallness is dominant ('overrules') the gene for shortness.

genes in sex cells of parent plants

tall   tall   tall   tall

Below: When two of the offspring are cross-fertilized (see below) they produce – on the average – three tall offspring for every one short offspring. Two of the tall plants have one gene for shortness but this is "overruled" by the dominant gene for tallness.

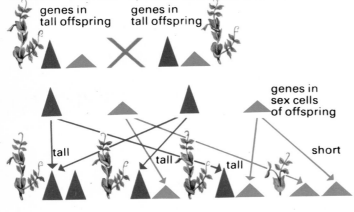

genes in tall offspring   genes in tall offspring

genes in sex cells of offspring

tall   tall   tall   short

offspring had short stems. You can find out more about how this happened in the diagrams on page 114.

Mendel did many experiments with different combinations of characteristics in his pea plants. In every case he got the same results. He worked out several basic rules of heredity (which are called Mendel's Laws). They have since been found to apply to other plants and also to animals.

Mendel's Laws

1. The characteristics of an organism are passed on from one generation to another by definite particles, which Mendel called *factors*. Today we call them *genes*.

2. The genes normally exist in pairs, which are alternative versions of the same genetic instruction. One of each pair of genes comes from the male parent and the other comes from the female parent.

3. The genes of a pair may be dominant or recessive to each other. *Dominant* genes always have an effect on the individual, even if only one gene is present. But two *recessive* genes have to be present before they have an effect. So some genes can be present in plants and animals without having an effect on their characteristics.

Where are the Genes?

A few years after Mendel had carried out his researches, biologists concluded that the genes are in the nucleus of every cell, carried on structures called *chromosomes*. The name means "color body." Chromosomes were given this name because they take up colored stains easily when biologists prepare cells for study under the microscope.

The chromosomes of all animals and plants exist in pairs. Each chromosome of a pair contains alternative versions of the same genes carried by its partner. A human cell has 23 pairs of chromosomes, a chicken cell 18 pairs, a mouse cell 10 pairs and a fruit fly cell 4 pairs. Biologists have done much of their research into genetics on a fruit fly called *Drosophila*. This is a convenient animal to use because it breeds rapidly (it has a lifespan of about 10 days) and it has a range of distinctive characteristics that can be used in breeding experiments.

You can find out more about genes and how they work on the next four pages.

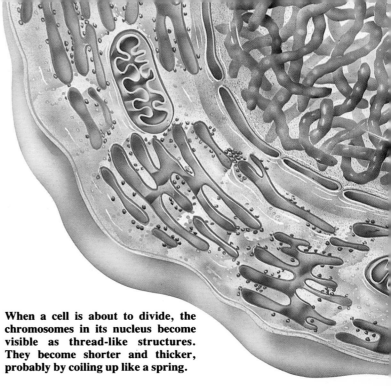

When a cell is about to divide, the chromosomes in its nucleus become visible as thread-like structures. They become shorter and thicker, probably by coiling up like a spring.

CHROMOSOMES AND GENES

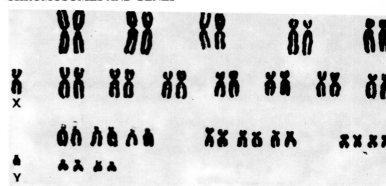

Above: The 46 chromosomes of a man, arranged in their 23 pairs. The X and Y sex chromosomes are named after their shape.
Below: Part of a giant chromosome from the salivary gland of the fruit fly, *Drosophila*. Many of the bands are the site of one or more genes.

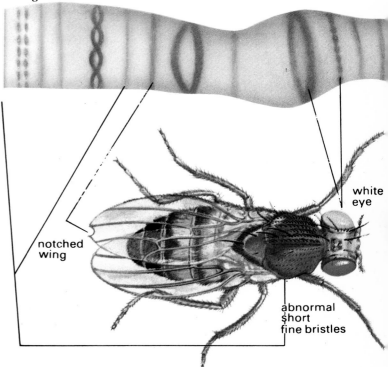

white eye

notched wing

abnormal short fine bristles

Life's Data Bank

The body of anyone reading this book is made of about 100,000,000,000,000 cells. Each cell contains the same set of plans for making a human being and keeping its body working. The plans are in the form of coded instructions (genes) on the chromosomes in the nucleus of every cell. The instructions were present in the fertilized egg cell that all humans develop from. They were copied and passed on to each new cell as the human being grew and developed. You can find out how the instructions are copied on pages 118-119 and on these two pages you can see what happens to the chromosomes that carry the instructions when a cell divides.

Switching Off the Genes

Although every cell in an organism contains all the instructions for making and controlling the characteristics of that organism, it uses only those instructions it needs to carry out its particular job in the body. The rest of the genetic instructions are somehow "switched off." How this happens is one of the greatest puzzles of biology but it may be connected with the position of the cell in the body.

Mitosis – Making Identical Cells

When a plant or animal is growing and developing from a fertilized egg cell, all its cells divide to produce the cells that go to make up its tissues and organs. In a fully-grown organism only some of the cells continue to divide. This process of cell division is called *mitosis*. Each chromosome copies itself, then the nucleus divides into two and finally the whole cell splits into two identical cells.

CREATING IDENTICAL CHROMOSOMES

The diagrams below show the main stages in the process of cell division called *mitosis*. This produces new body cells in plants and animals and each division forms two new cells, which are identical to the original cell.

Centromere

1. The cell before division begins. The chromosomes become visible in the nucleus. Only two pairs of chromosomes are shown for simplicity.

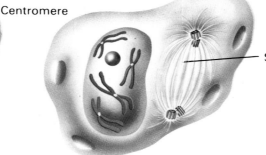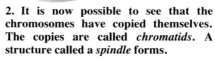

Spindle

2. It is now possible to see that the chromosomes have copied themselves. The copies are called *chromatids*. A structure called a *spindle* forms.

3. The membrane around the nucleus breaks down and the chromosomes move toward the center of the spindle.

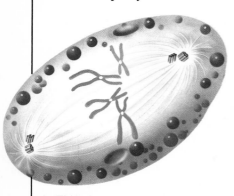

4. The chromosomes line up at the center of the spindle and attach to the spindle fibers.

5. The two chromatids in each double chromosome separate and move to opposite ends of the spindle. The cell begins to divide.

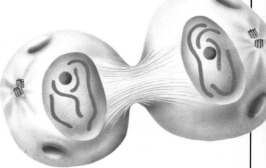

6. Two new nuclear membranes form around each group of chromosomes and the cell divides into two.

Meiosis – Making Different Cells

When reproductive cells (sperm, pollen and egg cells) are produced, a special type of cell division takes place. This is called *meiosis*. Meiosis halves the number of chromosomes so that when two reproductive cells join to form a new plant or animal, it will have the same number of chromosomes as its parent. This is how each species keeps the same number of chromosomes from one generation to another.

But meiosis does far more than halve the number of chromosomes. The chromosomes also cross over each other and swop genes before the cell divides. This process reshuffles the genetic instructions so that each reproductive cell has its own unique combination of instructions. (So, for example, no two sperm cells will have exactly the same combination of genes.) Two of these unique cells join to form a new individual in sexual reproduction (see pages 56-59), which mixes up the genetic instructions even further. This explains why no two people (except for identical twins) are exactly alike.

The variations caused by this system of cell division are very important in the evolution of living things. Darwin's idea of the "survival of the fittest" (see page 107) would be meaningless if there was not a range of genetically different organisms for nature to "select" from. The environment can only weed out the less well adapted individuals if there is plenty of variation in a species.

Below: The human reproductive cells formed in meiosis have either an X or a Y sex chromosome. If two cells with X chromosomes join together at fertilization, a female will develop. A fertilized cell with one X and one Y sex chromosome will develop into a male. The X and Y chromosomes carry different instructions. For example, the gene for normal color vision is carried only on the X chromosome. If males have a defective gene for color vision on their one X chromosome, they will be color blind. But females have to inherit the defective gene on both their X chromosomes to be color blind. This is because the gene is recessive and is "overruled" if they have a normal gene (which is dominant) on one of their X chromosomes.

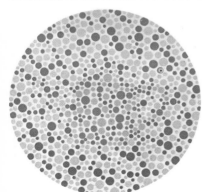

If you have normal color vision, you will be able to see a teapot in this picture.

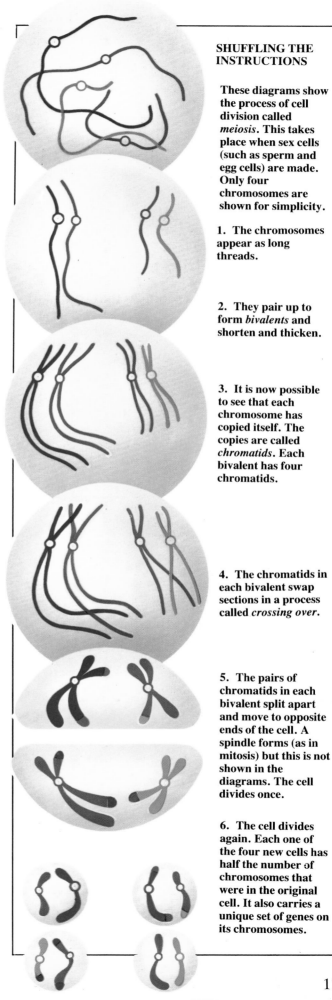

SHUFFLING THE INSTRUCTIONS

These diagrams show the process of cell division called *meiosis*. This takes place when sex cells (such as sperm and egg cells) are made. Only four chromosomes are shown for simplicity.

1. The chromosomes appear as long threads.

2. They pair up to form *bivalents* and shorten and thicken.

3. It is now possible to see that each chromosome has copied itself. The copies are called *chromatids*. Each bivalent has four chromatids.

4. The chromatids in each bivalent swap sections in a process called *crossing over*.

5. The pairs of chromatids in each bivalent split apart and move to opposite ends of the cell. A spindle forms (as in mitosis) but this is not shown in the diagrams. The cell divides once.

6. The cell divides again. Each one of the four new cells has half the number of chromosomes that were in the original cell. It also carries a unique set of genes on its chromosomes.

117

Making Proteins to Control Life

Since the origin of life about 3.5 billion years ago, each generation of living things has had to copy its genetic instructions and pass them on to the next generation. On these two pages you can find out more about the instructions themselves, how they work and how they are copied.

Genes – the Coded Instructions

A gene is a section of a remarkable molecule called *deoxyribonucleic acid* or DNA for short. DNA is found in the chromosomes in the nucleus of cells. It controls the characteristics of living things by means of a chemical code of instructions. DNA is found in all living things, which suggests that all life on earth may have had a common origin.

The structure of DNA was discovered in the early 1950s by two scientists, Francis Crick and James Watson, who were working at the University of Cambridge, England. They received the Nobel Prize for their achievement, which was one of the most important contributions to biology since the work of Darwin and Mendel.

Crick and Watson showed that the structure of the DNA molecule looks rather like a twisted ladder. The shape is called a *double helix*. The rungs of the ladder are coded instructions and the sides are made of sugar and phosphate molecules. The coded instructions are written with four chemical building blocks – adenine (A), thymine (T), guanine (G) and cytosine (C). These are called *bases* and they make up a four letter alphabet. They can only pair up in a certain way. A can only pair with T and G can only pair with C. A pair of bases is called a *nucleotide*.

The order of the nucleotides along the DNA strand spells out the instructions for the different characteristics of organisms. One gene may consist of up to a thousand pairs of bases. A bacterium called *E.coli* has about 4,000 base pairs on its single chromosome. No one knows how many base pairs are needed to spell out the coded instructions for a human being. But it may be more than ten million.

HOW DNA IS COPIED

The two strands of a DNA molecule are normally linked together. But when a cell is about to divide into two (see pages 116-117), the strands unwind so the molecule can make a copy of itself. All the DNA molecules in the nucleus of a cell are copied so the two new cells contain the same DNA as the original cell.

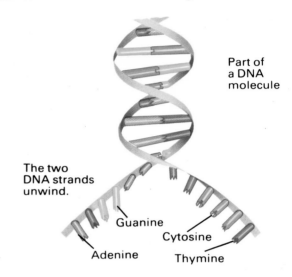

Part of a DNA molecule

The two DNA strands unwind.

Guanine
Cytosine
Adenine
Thymine

When a DNA molecule makes a copy of itself, it first splits down the middle of the ladder. Some of the four building blocks that make up the rungs of the ladder are present in the nucleus. They are called adenine (A), thymine (T), guanine (G), and cytosine (C). A always links to T and G always links to C. The spare building blocks match up with their partners on the separated strands. This produces an exact copy of the original molecule.

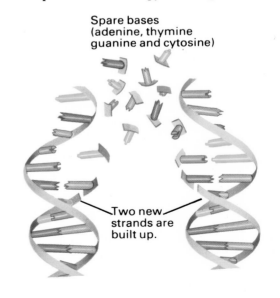

Spare bases (adenine, thymine guanine and cytosine)

Two new strands are built up.

In this way, two molecules of DNA are built up, each identical to the original one.

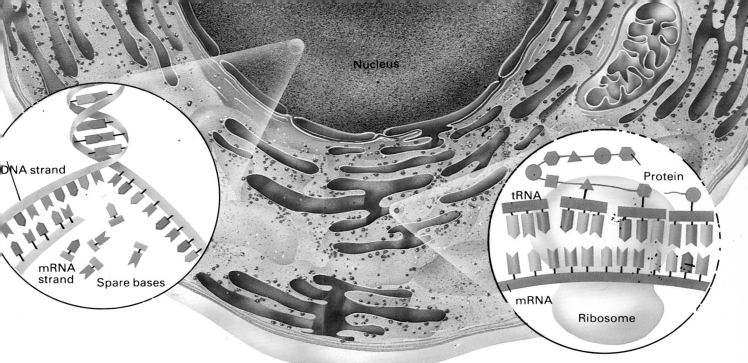

Nucleus

DNA strand

mRNA strand

Spare bases

tRNA

Protein

mRNA

Ribosome

HOW DNA MAKES A PROTEIN

To make a protein, a DNA molecule first makes a copy of a small section of itself, which is like an order for making a particular protein. The copy is in the form of a molecule called *ribonucleic acid* or RNA for short. RNA is similar to DNA but has only one strand, a molecule called uracil in place of thymine and a sugar called ribose in place of deoxyribose. It is called messenger RNA (mRNA) because it passes out of the nucleus and carries the message for making a protein to a ribosome. mRNA threads through a ribosome and its message is read by another form of RNA called transfer RNA (tRNA). tRNA molecules carry amino acids to the ribosome, where they link up to form a protein.

How Does the DNA Code Work?

The coded instructions on the DNA molecules control the production of proteins. And proteins control the characteristics of organisms.

Proteins are the most common chemicals in living things. Each cell in your body contains at least 10,000 different kinds of protein. The most important proteins are the enzymes that control the rate of chemical reactions in cells, without being used up themselves. They are vital to life.

Proteins are made of twenty different units called amino acids. The order of the amino acids determines the type of protein. But how does the four letter alphabet of the DNA code spell out the messages for twenty different amino acids? The four letters are actually read in groups of three. (For example, the order of bases TAG-CATACT would be read as the three words TAG, CAT and ACT.) There are 64 possible ways of arranging four letters in groups of three. (Try working this out for yourself.) Only 20 messages are needed for the amino acids, plus a message that means "stop, this is the end of the message for one protein." So some of the 64 possible messages are not used while others appear to have the same meaning.

How Does DNA Make Proteins?

DNA remains in the safety of the nucleus. But proteins are made on structures called *ribosomes*, which are in the cytoplasm of the cell (see page 10). A copy is made of a section of a DNA molecule and this is sent out of the nucleus to a ribosome. There it controls the production of a particular protein. You can see how this complex process works in the diagram at the top of the page.

Changing the DNA Code

Very rarely, the DNA code is changed in some way. This changes the proteins that are made and so alters the characteristics of organisms. Such changes play a part in the evolution of living things.

Changes to the DNA code are called *mutations*, after the latin word *mutare*, which means to change. There are two main sorts of mutation. One is a mistake in the code itself, such as one base pair being replaced by a different one. This takes place when DNA reproduces itself. The other involves changes in the positions of large pieces of DNA, which take place during cell division, especially in meiosis (see page 117). Many mutations are harmful causing the death of the organism. Other mutations have only slight effects or no noticeable effect at all. Some cause obvious changes in the organism.

The Origin of Life

One of the greatest mysteries in biology is how life first arose on the earth about 3.5 billion years ago. What is the chemical link between the build-up of organic molecules (which have been made by scientists in experiments) and the first systems of molecules that reproduced themselves? We may never really understand this gap between the living and the nonliving. One thing that seems certain to most biologists is that all life on earth had a common origin. The chemistry of life is very complex, yet it is the same in all existing lifeforms. And all life on earth uses the same language (the DNA code) to transmit its characteristics from generation to generation.

When scientists analyzed living matter they discovered an intriguing fact. Life is formed from the most common elements in the universe. The human body, for example, is made of mainly hydrogen (the most common element), oxygen, nitrogen, carbon and phosphorus. (Actually we are about three-fourths water, which is why we have so much hydrogen and oxygen in our bodies.) The elements of life were therefore abundant before the origin of life. So how could they have joined together to form the molecules that make up living things?

Scientists at the Ames Research Center in California have used this apparatus to recreate the sort of conditions in the earliest atmosphere on earth. In the experiment, a mixture of ammonia, methane, water vapor, nitrogen and hydrogen is heated by electric discharges. Amino acids – vital to all life on earth – are formed.

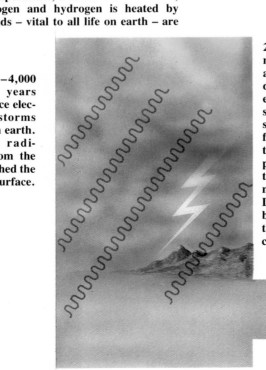

1. 4,600–4,000 million years ago, fierce electrical storms raged on earth. Lethal radiation from the sun reached the earth's surface.

Electrical storms

2. About 4,000 million years ago, water condensed on the earth's cooling surface. Dissolved gases from the primitive atmosphere reacted to form organic molecules. During the next billion years the first living cells evolved.

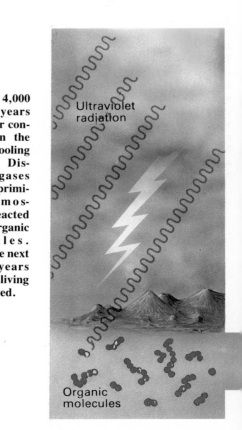

Ultraviolet radiation

Organic molecules

Scientists have carried out many experiments which show how the molecules of life could have formed in the sort of atmosphere the earth would have had about four billion years ago. This is called a *primordial atmosphere*, which means "existing at the beginning." Professor Stanley Miller of the University of Chicago was the first to experiment with a primordial atmosphere in 1953. He put together the "atmosphere" in his laboratory apparatus and passed an electrical current through it. And some of the molecules of life formed in his apparatus.

Many scientists have successfully repeated Professor Miller's experiments. Different combinations of gases have been used to represent the earth's primordial atmosphere and different forms of energy have been used to trigger the production of organic molecules. In the primordial earth atmosphere, the energy for the buildup of complex molecules could have come from lightning, radiation, volcanic eruptions or even meteorite impacts. Experiments show that the molecules of life do not form in the presence of oxygen. So they could not form in today's atmosphere. But scientists accept that the earth's first atmosphere was mostly hydrogen.

The Chemistry of Early Life

Most biologists believe that life almost certainly began in water, either in the sea or on the shoreline. But what sort of molecules would have been needed for life to arise?

The only molecules that can carry a vast amount of coded information and copy themselves are the nucleic acids. These are the DNA and RNA molecules, which you can find out more about on pages 118-119. Nucleic acids would have had to form before the origin of life.

Amino acids, the units that proteins are made of, would also have been essential. Proteins are the structural materials of life. The enzymes that control all the vital chemical reactions of life are also proteins.

Nucleic acids and proteins each provide what the other needs in a living system. The nucleic acids can copy themselves but they would have had to produce the codes for proteins to be made. So these two chemicals somehow had to come together to produce life. When such systems began to copy (reproduce) themselves in a stable way, life would have begun. The first systems may have been unstable and life may have had to form several times before the right molecules came together in the right way.

We may never know how molecules fitted together to produce the first life. But we know that amino acids link up to form proteins. And we can guess how proteins and nucleic acids may have come together to form a functioning, self-copying system.

Right: Blue-green algae as they appear under a microscope. Relatives of these organisms probably survived on earth some 2.5 billion years ago.

Below: The diagram below shows how living cells could have evolved from simple to more complex types. 1 and 2 – A simple bacterial cell becomes incorporated in another cell in a form of symbiosis (see pages 88-89). In time it becomes a part of the larger cell called a mitochondrion (see page 10). 3 and 4 – In a similar way, a cell of an alga becomes incorporated in a second cell. It evolves into a structure called a chloroplast (see page 11). 5 – More complex cells eventually formed with both mitochondria and chloroplasts and these became the ancestors of plants and animals.

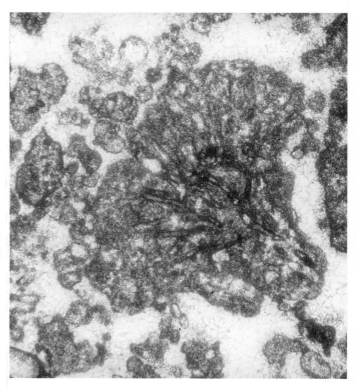

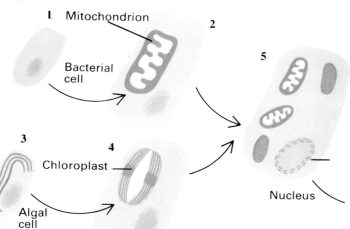

Is There Life on Other Planets?

Scientists have long wondered about the possible existence of life on other plants in our solar system. Does the surface of Mars, the sea of Saturn's moon Titan or the dense water layer of Jupiter's atmosphere shelter life of any kind?

Mars and Venus

Before the space age, astronomers knew that Mars was cold with only a thin atmosphere because they could see right to its surface. But when the polar ice melted in summer, Mars seemed to darken as if vegetation was growing on its surface. Then American spacecraft surveyed Mars at close quarters and found that there was no vegetation. The Viking Landers the U.S. sent to the surface of Mars recorded some very unusual chemistry. But most scientists think there is no life on Mars.

Before any spacecraft reached Venus, some astronomers suggested that Venus might have steamy jungles on its surface. But Soviet spacecraft which landed on Venus found that there was no water there. In fact the surface of Venus is several times hotter than boiling water. Even the most heat-resistant lifeforms would go up in smoke.

Jupiter and Titan

Jupiter is a gas giant with no solid surface. Observations have shown that it is a vast cauldron of organic chemistry. This may be similar to the pre-life chemistry of the earth.

Another possible place for life is Saturn's moon Titan, which is one of the most fascinating places in the solar system. Titan's water is locked up as ice – the surface temperature is minus 356°F. The surface is completely hidden

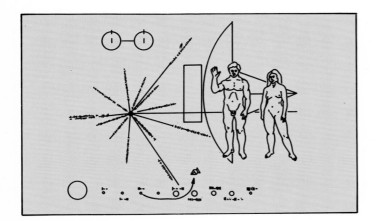

Left: American astronomers Carl Sagan and Frank Drake of Cornell University worked out this message. It is designed to tell any beings that may exist on other worlds the kind of creatures who sent it and where they are located in our galaxy. It is on a plaque carried by Pioneer 10, now on its way out of the solar system.

Below left: This photograph of the earth's moon was taken in 1968 by the Apollo 8 astronauts. There is no life on the moon because it has no water and no atmosphere. A planet without an atmosphere has a huge difference between night and day temperatures.
Below right: The Apollo 8 astronauts also took this photograph of the earth from moon orbit. In the bottom of the picture are the lunar highlands.

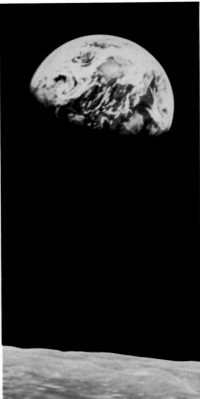

Below: The surface of Mars as seen in the photographs taken by the Viking Landers.
One of the Landers is shown in the photograph to the left.

Above: The dense, cloudy atmosphere of Venus is mainly composed of carbon dioxide and nitrogen. It contains little water. Soviet spacecraft have shown that the suface is several times hotter than boiling water.

Below: A close-up of the swirling gas clouds on Jupiter. The surface clouds are about minus 184°F (120°C). But the atmosphere get warmer and denser with depth.

Above: The United States' two Viking Landers were the only spacecraft launched especially to detect evidence of life on Mars. Each landed and tested the soil in special experiments. This revealed some very unusual chemistry but most scientists do not think this is caused by an unknown type of life. Future landings may provide definite answers.

Below: The surface of Saturn's moon Titan is completely hidden by an orange atmosphere. This is 50 percent denser than the earth's atmosphere. Future spacecraft will attempt to find out if there is life on Titan. It would have to function without water, unlike life on earth.

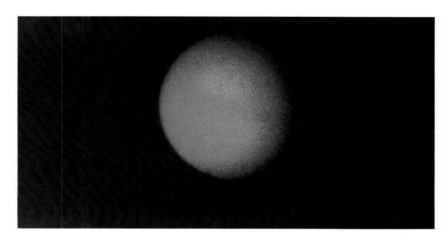

by an orange atmosphere, which is 50 percent denser than the earth's atmosphere. There is good evidence to believe that Titan may be covered by a sea of ethane and methane gases a mile deep.

The radiation reaching Titan's atmosphere from Saturn and the Sun produces chemical reactions that form organic molecules in the atmosphere. These then fall through the atmosphere and into the sea. This may have been going on for about four billion years. Such molecules probably formed in a sea of water on earth about four billion years ago. Could there be a form of life on Titan that can exist in a sea probably made of liquid ethane and methane? Future spacecraft to Titan will attempt to answer this question.

Limits to Life

Scientists interested in the remote possibility that life exists elsewhere in the solar system have to consider the range of conditions in which life can survive. Recent discoveries have shown that this range is greater than anyone imagined.

One of the best examples of life in extreme conditions is of bacteria collected from superheated water that pours from a vent in the seabed of the Pacific Ocean. The bacteria there live in a temperature of 680°F. Scientists are uncertain how living matter can hold together under such intense heat. Now that the known temperature range for life on earth has been increased, biologists can look again at some ideas about life in rather hot places, such as the water layer in Jupiter's atmosphere.

The Biotechnology Revolution

Revolutionary changes to the world we live in (such as airplanes, computers and plastics) have been brought about by discoveries in the physical sciences. But the rapidly growing understanding of genetics and the biochemistry of cells could have an ever greater impact on our lives in the years ahead. The science of using this new knowledge for practical purposes is called *biotechnology*. Many people see it as a new industrial revolution.

There is nothing new about some aspects of biotechnology. People have used microbes (such as bacteria and yeasts) in brewing, baking, and wine and cheese making for thousands of years. These processes take advantage of the fact that microbes naturally produce substances which are of value to people.

Genetic Engineering

But research in the sciences of genetics and molecular biology has sparked off a new interest in biotechnology. It is now possible for scientists to give bacteria genes (see pages 118-119) from other organisms, including humans. Genes are chemical codes of instructions for making particular proteins. The foreign genes (plus the proteins that are produced as a result of their instructions) are reproduced billions of times as the bacteria grow and divide. So the bacteria can be used as "factories" for making proteins they would not normally produce. Some of the proteins, such as human growth hormone and interferon, are difficult to obtain in other ways and therefore very valuable.

Bacteria are so abundant and have such a wide variety of genes that they can be used to process almost any substance. For example, some bacteria have genes which allow them to eat oil slicks and break down other toxic wastes. And special bacteria are now being produced by genetic engineering to solve problems of pollution.

Scientists can also use the techniques of genetic engineering to change the genes in domesticated animals and plants. This may help to make them grow faster or larger or be more resistant to diseases. Plants can also be given new genes to help them survive frost and

Medicine and health Antibiotics, hormones, interferon, vaccines. Research on genetic diseases.

Food and agriculture Wine, bread, cheese. Breeding new crops and farm animals.

Processing wastes Pollution and sewage.

Recovering metals from rock and seawater.

Energy production Biological fuels.

Enzyme engineering for chemical reactions.

Mathematics and Computer technology

Chemical and process Engineering

Biochemistry

Applied microbiology

Genetics

Chemistry

Above: The biotechnology tree in this diagram shows the main uses of biotechnology in the modern world.

Below: The white paste on this large drum is made of thousands of millions of bacterial cells. They are used to make enzymes in the production of penicillin antibiotics.

124

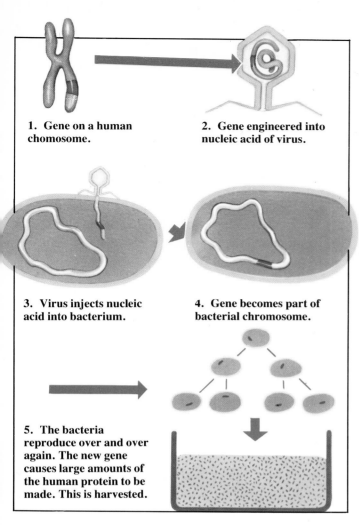

1. Gene on a human chomosome.

2. Gene engineered into nucleic acid of virus.

3. Virus injects nucleic acid into bacterium.

4. Gene becomes part of bacterial chromosome.

5. The bacteria reproduce over and over again. The new gene causes large amounts of the human protein to be made. This is harvested.

Above: Microbes such as bacteria can now be made to carry the genes of other species, including humans. The genes carry instructions for making proteins, such as enzymes and antibodies. So bacteria can be used to produce large amounts of valuable proteins for use in industry and medicine.

Below: This is a virus that infects bacteria (a *bacteriophage*). It is magnified 1.2 million times. Such bacteriophages are used to carry pieces of genetic information from one organism to another in the process of genetic engineering.

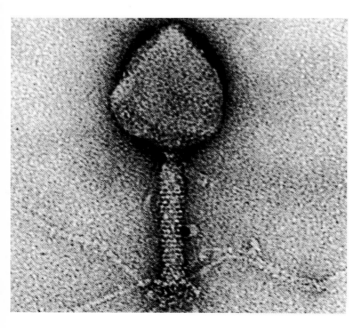

drought. Medical scientists hope eventually to be able to cure inherited diseases, such as *hemophilia*, by giving patients new genes.

Moving Genes Around

Genetic engineering in biotechnology involves putting new genes into an organism, usually a bacterium, so it can make proteins it has never made before. There are usually four main stages to this process:

1. Obtaining a piece of DNA which contains the chemical code of instructions (the gene) for making a particular substance. (Enzymes are used to "snip out" a section of DNA.)
2. Putting the gene into a microscopic organism, usually a bacterium.
3. Making the gene produce the foreign protein in its new home.
4. Collecting the new protein.

Plasmids – the Magic Circles

Carrier molecules called *vectors* are used to introduce the gene into its new home. (The word vector comes from the latin for "carrier" or "bearer.") Certain types of viruses can act as vectors and so can little circles of DNA called *plasmids*, which are produced by some bacteria. Plasmids often pass from one bacterium to another, even if they are different species. This is a natural process.

The plasmid ring can be opened up using a special enzyme, called a *restriction enzyme*. A piece of DNA from another species, such as a human being, can be "stitched into" the ring. When the plasmid enters a bacterium in the usual way, it carries the gene to its new home. There it causes the foreign protein to be made.

The bacterium most often used as a home for new genes is called *E. coli*. It was chosen partly because it had been studied for many years and a great deal was known about its biochemistry. Once a plasmid is inside an *E. coli* cell, it makes copies of itself. If it contains a human gene, then that gene is copied as well. When the bacterium grows and divides, a few of the plasmids pass to each new cell. Before long, one bacterium will have produced millions of descendants exactly like itself, all containing the protein made as a result of the new gene. A population of cells produced by one ancestor is called a *clone*. All the cells in a clone have the same genetic make-up.

Living Factories

The use of genetic engineering for industrial processes has several advantages. It allows microbes such as bacteria to change cheap raw materials into valuable products. They can produce substances that are difficult to make in other ways. The industrial processes involved use very little energy and work at low temperatures. This cuts down the production costs.

Hormones and Genetic Engineering

The hormone *insulin* controls the amount of sugar in the blood stream. It is needed to treat people suffering from diabetes who cannot make enough of the hormone. Insulin is extracted from the pancreas of pigs and cows but it can have some undesirable side effects. This is probably because it is not identical to human insulin and it is difficult to obtain as a pure product.

Now the human gene for making insulin has been put into the bacterium *E. coli* and commercial quantities of human insulin are

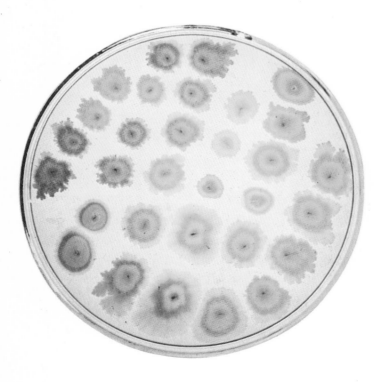

Above: The colonies of a bacterium called *Bacillus subtilis* in this photograph can be used as "factories" for making particular products. The red colonies are good producers and pink and gray are less suited. White colonies are non-producers. Techniques for identifying which bacteria are making the product are important in biotechnology.

being produced. In September 1982, insulin from bacteria became the first genetically engineered material to be licensed for use in humans.

Growth hormone is made in the pituitary, a small gland at the base of the brain. It stimulates growth and is needed to treat some children who do not grow to a normal height. It is extracted from the brains of sheep. But only 0.005 grams of pure growth hormone can be obtained from half a million sheep's brains. Today just nine quarts of bacteria can produce the same amount of growth hormone.

Interferon

Interferon, a protein made by our cells, helps other cells to resist the effect of invading viruses. It was given its name because it appeared to *interfere* with the spread of viral infections. Until recently, interferon was very difficult to produce. It was made in the laboratory by infecting human white blood cells with viruses. This stimulated them to produce interferon. But only small amounts are made by each cell and the interferon is difficult to separate from all the other materials. So interferon was a rare and expensive substance.

But it is now possible to make interferon in large quantities by giving bacteria the gene for one type of human interferon. It may be very useful in medical treatment in the future, for example in the treatment of some viral diseases and perhaps some cancers.

Vaccines

Vaccines contain dead or weakened forms of a virus, which is produced in animals or cells in the laboratory. Some of the virus proteins stimulate us to produce antibodies. The antibodies prepare our bodies to fight a real viral infection later on.

Vaccines can now be produced by genetic engineering. Scientists take the virus genes that code for the specific proteins that stimulate the production of antibodies. The genes are inserted into bacteria. The bacteria then make the proteins in large quantities and these alone are used as a vaccine.

This technique allows manufacturers of vaccines to avoid handling dangerous microbes. It also reduces the risk that vaccines contain live viruses. It may provide protection against diseases such as influenza and rabies, that cannot be fought by normal vaccines.

Agriculture and Genetic Engineering

Agricultural plants have been given new genes in attempts to make them disease- and frost-resistant. And agricultural scientists are working to produce crops, especially cereals, that do not need fertilizers.

Most plants get the nitrogen they need for growth from the soil. So to grow better crops, nitrogen has to be provided in the form of fertilizers. But fertilizers are expensive, especially for third world countries. Yet there is plenty of nitrogen available in the atmosphere, which is 80 percent nitrogen. And certain plants, such as peas and beans, are able to use this nitrogen in a process called *nitrogen-fixing*. Bacteria in the roots of these plants extract nitrogen gas from the air and turn it into a form the plant can use.

Biologists would like to use the techniques of genetic engineering to make it possible for bacteria to live in the roots of crop plants and fix nitrogen for them. They are even working on techniques to give the nitrogen-fixing genes from bacteria to the crop plants so that they could use nitrogen from the air.

Microbe Farms

Food can be grown very rapidly in the factory with the help of microorganisms. This food is called *single cell protein* (SCP).

Biotechnologists have been using bacteria, yeasts and algae to produce food on a very small scale for some years. The microbes feed on some unwanted and abundant substances and multiply rapidly. The microbes themselves are made of proteins, carbohydrates, vitamins and minerals so they serve as a source of food. Most of the food produced like this is fed to domestic animals but some has been produced for humans to eat.

There are two great advantages to using special microbes to produce food. One is that they can eat substances which are abundant but useless for feeding domestic animals. The other is that they can produce food at a faster rate than any other lifeform because they reproduce so rapidly. They do not take up valuable land and could provide a valuable source of food for the world's growing population in the future.

Above: Root nodules on a bean plant, which contain bacteria that can fix nitrogen from the air. Genetic engineers may one day be able to give plants nitrogen-fixing genes.

Below: One of the earliest forms of biotechnology – using yeast to make beer in a brewery. The frothy scum is caused by the action of the yeast on the malt.

Below: The bacteria in this blue-green culture are concentrating copper salts. Such organisms are used to recover copper from mining ores and wastes which contain very little copper. It would be too expensive to recover the copper by normal methods. Bacteria can also be used to extract silver and rare metals from seawater. One day this may become a major industrial operation.

Glossary

Algae The simplest of plants. They have a plant body but no root, stem or leaves. Algae may be single-celled or many-celled plants and range in size from the microscopic to seaweeds.

Amino acids The molecules that link up to make proteins. See *protein molecules*.

Ammonite Member of a very large group of prehistoric sea creatures. They were related to the cephalopods (the octopus and nautilus). The ammonites became extinct some 65 million years ago.

Amylase An enzyme which breaks up starch. The names of enzymes often end in "ase."

Androecium All the *stamens* in a flower.

Angiosperm A flowering plant, such as a daisy or buttercup. There are two groups of angiosperms – *monocotyledons* and *dicotyledons*. The word angiosperm means vessel seed – the seeds are protected inside an *ovary* as they grow. Angiosperms and *gymnosperms* are together known as the seed plants.

Annual rings Rings seen on the cut surface of logs and stems. They indicate the age of the tree. Stems grow from the center outward. Every year, the new *xylem* produced by *secondary thickening* produces one annual ring. Toward the center of each ring the cells are large and are made in spring when growth is most active. At the outside of the ring, the cells are smaller and are made later in the year. These cells form a darker band, so that each year's growth can easily be counted.

Antibiotic A substance produced by one living organism which is poisonous to another. The most famous antibiotic is penicillin which has been used for more than 40 years to kill disease-causing bacteria. Penicillin is produced by several species of the mold penicillium. Antibiotics are widespread in the world of microbes, but only about 50 different antibiotics have been found suitable for medical use.

Antibodies *Protein molecules* produced by the body to defend itself against invading microbes. Antibodies are also produced against toxins and surgical grafts from another person. This capacity of the body to reject foreign tissues is the main problem in transplant surgery.

Arachnids *Arthropods* that have eight legs in contrast to the insects which have six legs. Spiders and mites are the most common arachnids.

Arthropods Animals with outside skeletons and limbs that have many joints. Insects form by far the largest group of arthropods. Crabs, prawns and spiders are also examples of common arthropods.

Auxin A chemical hormone that affects the rate or direction of plant growth.

Bacillus A rod-shaped bacterium. A bacillus is responsible for tuberculosis.

Bacteriophage *Viruses* which infect bacteria. Bacteriophages are now used in genetic engineering to insert selected *DNA* in bacteria.

Biosphere The surface of the earth and the lower atmosphere where all living things are to be found. The biosphere includes all seas and oceans.

Biotechnology The use of biological knowledge for practical purposes.

Bulb A short underground stem wrapped in swollen leaf bases, for example, onion, daffodil. New plants can grow from its buds by *vegetative reproduction*.

Calyx A ring of *sepals* on the outside of a flower.

Cambium A *meristem* inside a plant stem or root. Cambium cells divide and grow to make the stem or root thicker, producing *secondary thickening*. There are two sorts of cambium. Vascular cambium makes new *xylem* and *phloem*. Cork cambium makes cork and secondary *cortex*, giving the stem a thick waterproof coat to replace the *epidermis*.

Cambrian The period in earth history which lasted from 570 to 500 million years ago. A widespread abundance of sea life is recorded by the fossils of the Cambrian age. All the major groups of animals were present at this time except the vertebrates.

Camouflage A disguise that hides a plant or animal from animals that eat it. Camouflage generally involves a pattern or color that makes the plant or animal difficult to see against its surroundings. For example, white feathers are camouflage for the ptarmigan, a bird that lives in snowy lands.

Carbon The "backbone" element of life. Each carbon atom has the capacity to join with four atoms. It can thus form chemical structures essential to all life.

Carbohydrates Organic molecules made of carbon, hydrogen and oxygen. Sugars and starch are the best known carbohydrates.

Carnivore An animal that feeds mainly on other animals. Carnivores, such as lions, are often called predators and the animals that they feed on are called their prey.

Carpel A structure in a flower where seeds are made. A flower may have one or more carpels. A carpel generally has a sticky tip (stigma) connected to a swollen base (*ovary*) by a stalk (style). The carpels are together known as the *gynoecium*.

Cartilage A tough whitish substance, flexible and strong, made of connective tissues. Gristle in meat is cartilage.

Cellulose Chains of carbohydrate molecules. Cellulose forms the walls of plant cells. It is a fibrous material and therefore not easily digested. Animals that live on plants, like cows and sheep, have specially evolved digestive systems to obtain maximum nourishment from cellulose.

Chlorophyll The green chemical pigment in plants. Chlorophyll traps energy from sunlight during *photosynthesis* and uses it to split water molecules into hydrogen and oxygen.

Chloroplast A microscopic sac in green plant cells where *photosynthesis* takes place. Inside a chloroplast are layers or disks called grana surrounded by a liquid called stroma. In the grana, chlorophyll captures energy from sunlight and splits water molecules into hydrogen and oxygen. In the stroma, hydrogen and carbon dioxide are combined to make *carbohydrates*.

Chromosome Rod-shaped structures visible in the nuclei of cells when they are about to divide lengthwise. It has been known for a long time that the chromosomes carry the chemical code of instructions that controls life. (See *DNA*, *genetic* and *nucleic acids*).

Coelenterates The group of animals containing sea-anemones, jellyfish and corals. All live in water and most in the sea. Of the many-celled animals the coelenterates are the simplest in structure. They are the simplest form of life to have nerve cells. The coelenterates have been a very successful lifeform. Their ancestors (similar to today's animals) can be found in the fossil record of more than 500 million years ago.

Collagen A fibrous protein. It is one of the main materials which bind cells and animal tissues together. Leather is the "fixed" collagen of the skin.

Cone A reproductive structure of a typical *gymnosperm*. The woody scales of a cone are basically modified leaves. Each scale can produce reproductive cells. Cones are either male or female. Male cones produce *pollen*. They are small and do not live long. Female cones are larger and take up to three years to produce seeds. In animals, cones are light sensitive cells in the eye.

Corm A swollen underground stem such as in a crocus. It contains stored food, and new plants can grow from its buds by *vegetative reproduction*.

Corolla A ring of petals in a flower, above the *calyx*. The word corolla means crown, and the petals are often the showiest part of a flower.

Cortex The area of packing cells between the *vascular bundles* and the *epidermis* in a plant stem or root. In animals, the cortex is the outer layer of the brain or kidney.

Cotyledon A leaf in a seed. A cotyledon becomes the first leaf of the *embryo* plant, and may be quite different from all the other leaves. Cotyledons store food for the embryo plant. Only *angiosperms* and *gymnosperms* have cotyledons.

Crustaceans A large group of the arthropods. Most crustaceans live in water. Shrimps, crabs and water-fleas are common examples.

Cuticle The waterproof outer skin of a plant leaf or stem, on top of the *epidermis*. The cuticle is transparent and is not made of cells.

Cytoplasm Everything enclosed by the cell membrane except the nucleus. Cytoplasm was a convenient description of the contents of cells at a time when it was not possible to know what cells actually contained. But cytoplasm is far more than fluid within the cell. It contains numbers of working molecules (*enzymes*), coded plans and instructions (carried by RNA), assembly units for proteins (ribosomes), energy generators (*mitochondria*) and other components of considerable complexity.

Deciduous A plant that regularly sheds all its leaves. Deciduous plants usually lose their leaves at the end of the growing season, before the winter. Many *angiosperms* such as oak, beech and ash trees are deciduous. Larch is one of the few *gymnosperms* that is deciduous.

Decomposer An animal or fungus that feeds on the dead remains or waste material of other living things. Decomposers break down their food into simple raw materials that can be reused by plants.

DNA (short for deoxyribonucleic acid) This chemical carries the *genetic* code for all organisms, except some *viruses*. The code determines the form, development and behavior pattern of an organism. DNA is part of the *chromosomes* which exist within the nuclei of cells.

Diatom A single-celled green alga with a silica case made of two halves that fit together, one inside the other, like a box. Diatoms are the main organisms of *plankton*.

Dicotyledon A flowering plant with two *cotyledons* in its seed. Dicotyledons have broad leaves with veins in a net-like pattern. Their stems can grow thicker as well as longer, and the *vascular bundles* are arranged in a ring. The flowers have petals and other parts in fours or fives. Dicotyledons include all broad-leaved trees and most shrubs and herbaceous plants.

Dinosaur A member of the major group of reptiles in earth history. Their extinction some 65 million years ago is a biological mystery.

Drupe A fruit with one hard stone surrounded by soft flesh and skin. The seed is inside the stone. Cherries, plums and peaches are examples of drupes. A blackberry is several small drupes joined together.

E.coli A type of bacteria widely used in research.

Echinoderms A group of animals that includes starfish, which is distinct from other animal groups. Echinoderms are different from other lifeforms in their five-fold symmetry. Evidence from living animals and fossils indicates that their closest relatives were the distant ancestors of the *vertebrates*.

Electron micoscope A microscope which enables us to see specimens by beams of electrons instead of light. The magnification obtained is far greater than is possible with the best optical microscopes.

Embryo The youngest stage of a new individual, which develops from fertilized egg cells. The embryo is undeveloped.

Endosperm A food supply inside a seed. Grain seeds and oil seeds, such as linseed, have a large endosperm. Some seeds have no endosperm and store food in *cotyledons* instead. Endosperm contains chemical substances that control the growth of the developing seed.

Enzymes These are proteins made by the "machinery" of the cell. Enzymes greatly increase the rates of chemical reactions within the cell. The chemistry of life would not be possible without enzymes.

Epidermis A single layer of cells just below the surface of plant stems or leaves. With the *cuticle*, it provides a tough skin. In animals, the epidermis is the outer layer of skin.

Epiphyte A plant that grows on the surface of another plant, but is not a *parasite*. For example, mosses growing on tree trunks are epiphytes. The word epiphyte means "on top of a plant."

Ethane An odorless gas at normal temperatures. Ethane (C_2H_6) is an organic molecule and a hydrocarbon because it is composed of both hydrogen and carbon.

Evergreen A plant that keeps its leaves all the year round. Most *gymnosperm* trees such as pine and spruce are evergreen.

Food chain A sequence of events when a *herbivore* eats a plant, and then a *carnivore* eats the herbivore. This is a 3-link food chain. In a 4-link food chain a second carnivore eats the first carnivore. Food chains are nearly always part of a *food web*.

Food web Interconnecting *food chains*. Links between food chains occur when animals feed on different foods. There are usually many connections between food chains so that each link of a food chain is always part of a food web.

Fossil A permanent record of a prehistoric organism. A fossil usually consists of mineral material which has replaced the original tissues of the organism. Often only fragments of fossilized parts of an animal or plant are found.

Frond The leaf of a fern.

Fruit The ripe *ovary* of a flower containing the seed. A fruit such as a lupine, that dries out and splits open to shoot the seeds out is called dehiscent. A fruit such as a poppy that releases the seeds some other way is called indehiscent.

Fruiting body A plant structure that makes *spores*.

Gametes The male and female sex cells. These may be sperm and ova in animals, or *pollen* and egg-cells in seed plants.

Gene A unit which determines an inherited characteristic of an organism. The characteristic may or may not be expressed (show itself in a particular organism). Genes are made of *DNA* and are part of the *chromosomes* which exist in the nucleus of the cell.

Genetic Concerned with *genes* and heredity. (See *DNA*, *nucleic acids* and *chromosomes*).

Genetic engineering The manipulation (engineering) of the *genes* for practical purposes. Genes that instruct the machinery of the cell to make a wanted protein are put into another organism, such as a bacterium, to produce that product in quantity.

Genus The classification which includes the most closely related species. A genus may contain one or many different species. We belong to the genus *Homo* and the species *sapiens*.

Germination The process in which a seed starts to grow. There are two different sorts of germination in flowering plants. In plants with hypogeal germination, such as broad beans, the *cotyledons* stay under the soil. In plants with epigeal germination, such as sunflowers, the cotyledons grow out of the seed and above the ground.

Glands An organ or collection of cells which produce one or more special chemicals. These are released through vessels to either the inside or to the outside of the organism. Glands are associated with such processes as the digestion of food and the release of sweat. Some glands in animals secrete hormones into the blood stream (see *hormones*).

Grooming An activity of an animal to keep its skin or coat, or another individual's skin or coat, in good condition. Grooming removes dirt and pests.

Gymnosperm One of the cone-bearing plants or their close relatives. Gymnosperms make seeds but do not have flowers. The main group of gymnosperms are conifers, for example, larch, spruce and pine. The word gymnosperm means naked seed – the seeds develop from unprotected *ovules*. Gymnosperms and *angiosperms* are together known as the seed plants.

Gynoecium All the *carpels* in a flower.

Hemoglobin The molecule which carries oxygen in the red blood cells of *vertebrate* animals. Some *invertebrate* animals also have hemoglobin in their blood.

Hemophilia A *genetic* disorder which prevents blood from clotting. Hemophilia affects only males.

Herbivore An animal that feeds mainly on plants, for example, a grazing animal such as a cow or a sheep.

Hormones Chemicals that organisms produce in minute amounts but which can have dramatic effects on their life processes. Hormones play an important part in the lives of both plants and animals. Animal hormones usually go straight into the blood stream. A common hormonal effect is that produced by adrenaline which increases heart rate and raises blood pressure, producing a state of alertness and readiness for vigorous physical activity.

Inflorescence A group of flowers on one stalk.

Interferon A natural substance produced by cells to counter infections by *viruses*. Interferon inhibits the reproduction of viruses within infected cells.

Invertebrate All animals which do not possess a backbone, although we do not usually think of single-celled animals, like the amoeba, as invertebrates.

Liverwort A simple green plant related to a moss. Liverworts are mostly small and flat, with shoots simpler than those of a moss. They live in moist, shady places.

Lymph The same as blood *plasma* (colorless blood fluid without the red cells). Lymph drains from the tissues and enters the lymphatic system of vessels. These eventually lead to the vena cava, the main vein in all four-legged *vertebrates*, as well as humans.

Mammal An animal with a backbone which feeds its young on milk from mammary glands. Almost all mammals have hair or fur. Whales and dolphins have lost their fur during their evolution in the sea. All mammals maintain a constant body temperature (warm-blooded). The only other group of animals to maintain constant body temperature are birds. Man is the most advanced mammal, though whales and dolphins with their large brains must also be considered very advanced mammals.

Marsupials A form of *mammal* found mainly in Australasia which bears its young in a very immature state. Young kangaroos, for example, are only 4 cm (1½ inches) long at birth and must find their way into the mother's pouch where they fasten securely to a nipple. Not all marsupials have pouches.

Meiosis Cell division associated with the production of sex cells (sperm and ova). This process reduces the number of *chromosomes* in the nucleus by half. Thus, when male and female reproductive cells unite the number of chromosomes possessed by the species is restored.

Meristem A plant growing point. The cells in a meristem can divide so that the plant grows bigger. The main meristems are at the tip of each root and shoot. A meristem inside a plant is called *cambium*.

Methane A gas at normal temperatures, colorless, odorless and inflammable. Methane is an organic molecule and a hydrocarbon because it is composed of hydrogen and carbon (CH_4). Mixed with air, oxygen or water methane is highly explosive.

Micropyle A microscopic hole in the *ovule* of a flowering plant where the pollen tube enters after *pollination*. The micropyle can sometimes be seen as a small hole in a seed coat.

Migration A seasonal movement made by many birds, fish and mammals, often between breeding and feeding grounds. Animals migrate to make the best use of food and warmth.

Mitochondria Small rod-shaped bodies within cells. The mitochondria produce the energy needed by the cell to drive its life processes.

Mitosis Normal cell division in which exact copies of the *chromosomes* are made, one set of chromosomes going to each new cell before the old one finally divides.

Mollusks A large group of animals including snails, mussels, oysters and whelks. Mollusks have soft bodies and most have shells. The largest and most advanced of mollusks are the cephalopods: the octopuses and squid.

Monocotyledon A flowering plant with only one *cotyledon* in its seed. They have long, narrow leaves with veins growing side by side. Their stems can grow longer but not thicker, and the *vascular bundles* are scattered. The flowers have petals and other parts in threes. Monocotyledons include all grasses, palms and lilies.

Monotremes Egg-laying *mammals* which survive only in Australasia. They are the duckbilled platypus and the spiny anteater. The platypus spends its life in water, much like a duck. The anteater is like a hedgehog and feeds on insects. In prehistory there must have been many kinds of monotremes in between these two extreme examples.

Mutation A change in the *genes* (*DNA*) which produces an inherited change in the organism. Most mutations are changes in single genes.

Mycorrhiza Root-like threads of fungi that grow in close association with tree roots. Both the fungus and the tree seem to benefit from the relationship.

Natural selection The survival of members of a species best suited to live and reproduce in a given environment.

Nectar A sweet liquid produced by many flowering plants, generally from the base of the petals. Nectar is collected for food by insects and other animals that visit the flower.

Nucleic acids The DNA and RNA molecules. The unique structure of these molecules enables them to carry coded information. This information specifies and controls the form and development of all organisms. DNA holds the information within the cell nucleus. RNA carries copies of this information into the cell, where it is acted upon. (See also *DNA* and *chromosomes*).

Omnivore An animal that feeds on both plant and animal material. Human beings are omnivores.

Organic Refers to matter of which living things are made. As this is highly organized matter, scientists called it organic. At one time all organic substances came from living things. But in modern times many organic substances are made in the laboratory and factory.

Organic molecules In biology this refers to molecules formed by living organisms. However, a great range of organic molecules are now man-made for many different purposes. All organic molecules contain the element *carbon*.

Ovary The part of the female reproductive system in flowering plants and animals that makes egg cells. A ripe ovary in a flowering plant is a *fruit*.

Ovule An area containing an egg cell in seed plants. The ovule has one or more protective coats called integuments. In *angiosperms* an ovule is inside an *ovary*.

Palisade layer The layer of cells in a typical plant leaf that contains most of the *chloroplasts*. The palisade layer is just below the upper *epidermis* and gets more sunlight than the rest of the leaf.

Parasite A living thing that gets its food from another living thing without necessarily killing it.

Pesticide A chemical that is used to kill pests. Most pesticides are used to kill insects and are called insecticides. The use of pesticides must be carefully controlled so that *food webs* are not destroyed.

Phloem The food pipeline in plants. It is made up of rows of living cells called sieve tubes joined end to end, together with their support cells. Phloem is usually part of a *vascular bundle*.

Photosynthesis The process in which green plants use energy from sunlight to convert carbon dioxide and water to make their own food. Photosynthesis takes place in *chloroplasts*.

Pith An area of spongy packing cells in the center of a plant stem. Sometimes the pith is hollow.

Placenta The organ in the uterus of pregnant *mammals* to which the growing *embryo* is attached. The embryo receives food and oxygen through the blood system of the placenta while waste products travel in the blood in the opposite direction. All mammals that reproduce in this way are called placental mammals.

Plankton Microscopic plants and animals that live in great numbers in water. Plankton is the main source of food for many animals. Plankton that is mainly plants is called phytoplankton, and plankton that is mainly animals is called zooplankton.

Plasma (Blood plasma) The liquid part of blood. It contains all the important substances of blood but no blood cells.

Plasmid A section of *DNA*. Bacteria exchange plasmids as part of their natural behavior. Scientists use this capacity of bacteria to insert new DNA into organisms in research and *genetic engineering*.

Platelets Minute fragments in the blood which play an important part in the clotting and sealing of wounds.

Pleistocene The period in earth history from 1½ million years ago until 10 thousand years ago. During this time there were four ice ages and modern man (*Homo sapiens*) evolved.

Plumule The miniature shoot in a seed, part of the *embryo* plant.

Pollen Yellow dust produced by *gymnosperms* and *angiosperms*. Each particle of pollen – a

pollen grain – contains one male sex cell. Pollen grains must travel to a female sex cell in the *ovule* and fertilize it for seeds to grow. The journey to the ovule is called *pollination*.

Pollination The transfer of *pollen* from male *cones* or anthers of seed plants to an *ovule*. Pollen travels by air, water or animals, particularly insects. In *gymnosperms*, pollen lands directly on the naked ovule. In *angiosperms* the pollen lands on a special area called the stigma, above the *ovary*, and grows a tube down into the ovary.

Preen An activity of a bird to trim and clean its feathers, usually with its beak.

Protein molecules Living tissues are made of proteins. Proteins exist in an almost limitless number of different forms. The units of proteins are smaller molecules known as *amino acids*. There are some 20 different amino acid molecules in living proteins. The amino acids are formed into long chains which fold up into very complicated structures. The form of these structures is always exactly the same for any given protein. The structure of the human *hemoglobin* molecule, for example, is always the same, unless faulty. The structure of a protein molecule matches its task in the body.

Prothallus A small, flat disk that grows from the *spore* of a fern. The prothallus produces male and female sex cells that can grow into the main fern plant.

Protista A name given to all single-celled organisms whether animals, plants, fungi or bacteria.

Protozoa A name given to all single-celled animals.

Radicle The miniature root in a seed, part of the *embryo* plant.

Respiration This takes place within living cells where food is "burned" in the presence of oxygen to release energy.

Rhizome A swollen underground plant stem, such as in an iris. It contains stored food and can produce new plants from its buds by *vegetative reproduction*.

Savanna A dry grassy plain with few or no trees, in tropical regions.

Secondary thickening Cells produced from the *cambium* of many seed plants that make stems and roots grow thicker. Wood is mostly *xylem* cells produced by secondary thickening.

Segmented worms Worms, such as the earthworm, are made of a series of units (segments). Each segment is a similar structure both inside and outside. The structures of blood vessels and nerves, for example, are repeated in each segment.

Sepal A leaf-like structure that protects the bud of a flower. The sepals are together known as the *calyx*.

Sorus A small patch, generally brown, on the underside of a fern *frond* where *spores* are made. Each sorus contains several *sporangia*.

Species A group of organisms which resemble each other and interbreed. One species can seldom breed with another species, but there are a few exceptions to this rule. The species of plants, animals and other organisms therefore remain distinct.

Sponges The simplest of all many-celled animals. Sponges are composed of many cooperating cells but they have no system of nerves. They live attached to rocks or the seabed. Except for one family of sponges all live in the sea. Most sponges are supported by a skeleton. A bath sponge is the skeleton of a certain type of sponge.

Sporangium (pl. *sporangia*) A structure that makes *spores* in fungi, algae, mosses and ferns. In mosses, the sporangium is a special case with a lid and is called a capsule.

Spore A reproductive cell of a fungus, alga, moss or fern, capable of growing into a new plant. Some spores have tough protective coats that can survive periods of drought or cold. Some single-celled animals make spores to help them survive adverse conditions.

Stamen A structure that makes *pollen* in a flowering plant. Each stamen has a stalk (filament) and an anther, where the pollen is made. The stamens together are known as the *androecium*.

Stoma (pl. *stomata*) A small hole in the *epidermis* of a plant leaf that can open and close to control the flow of air and water vapor in and out of a leaf. Each stoma is controlled by two sausage-shaped cells in the epidermis, called guard cells.

Symbiosis The close association of two different kinds of organisms to their mutual benefit. Good examples are lichens which are formed of green algae and fungi. The algae use sunlight to make food while the fungi provide water and some protein.

Synapse The gaps between nerve cells across which nerve impulses pass. An impulse is changed from an electrical signal into a chemical and back into an electrical signal for the purpose of crossing a synapse. Such a substance is called a chemical transmitter.

Taxonomy The science of classifying living organisms.

Termite An insect that looks like an ant (but is in fact related to cockroaches), and that lives in large colonies. Some termites live in huge towers that they build out of mud. Most live in the tropics. Some grow special fungus gardens in their nests and use the fungus to add to their diet of vegetable matter.

Territory A patch of land defended by an animal against other members of the same species. Some animals hold territories all year round, others only at breeding time.

Transpiration Evaporation of water from the leaves of plants. Transpiration causes water to travel from the roots, up the stem and out through the leaves. Transpiration supplies all parts of the plant with water, which it uses to make food, and it helps the leaves and stems keep their shape.

135

Tropism A change in direction or rate of growth of a plant root or shoot in response to the environment. Tropisms are controlled by chemicals called *auxins*.

Tuber A rounded swelling at the end of an underground shoot or root. For example, a potato is a tuber. A tuber contains stored food and new plants can grow from its buds by *vegetative reproduction*.

Vaccination The introduction of dead or inactive bacteria or *viruses* into the blood stream. The presence of these are enough to cause the cells of our immune system to make *antibodies*. These antibodies will then protect us against future infections by the disease.

Vacuole A small drop of fluid within an animal cell. In plants vacuoles are larger, occupying most of the volume of the cell.

Vascular bundle A group of vessels, sieve tubes and supporting cells (*xylem* and *phloem*) that carry food and water around a plant.

Vegetative reproduction A process in which some plants can produce new plants from a small part of themselves without the need for flowers or seeds. *Rhizomes*, *tubers*, *bulbs* and *corms* are organs of vegetative reproduction.

Vertebrate An animal with a backbone. The backbone is sometimes called the vertebral column.

Virus A simply constructed system which only becomes alive when it enters a living cell. It then uses the "machinery" of the cell to make more viruses. Although viruses are a common cause of disease, they do not all cause disease. Viruses are so small that they can only be seen and studied with an *electron microscope*.

Vitamins Substances needed in minute amounts for the health of animals. Vitamins are different and unrelated substances.

Xylem The water pipeline in plants. In flowering plants xylem is made of rows of dead cells called vessels joined end to end. Xylem is usually part of a *vascular bundle*.

Yeasts Single-celled fungi of great practical value to man in the production of wine and beer and in baking.

Zygote A fertilized egg before it begins to divide and develop into a new organism. The cell resulting from a male and female cell coming together.

Index

Page numbers in italics refer to illustrations.

137

ACKNOWLEDGEMENTS
4 right Gene Cox; 5 center University of Birmingham; 8 left NASA, top right N.H.P.A, center right Brian Hawkes, bottom right P.Morris; 11 top Ann Ronan Picture Library; 12 top N.H.P.A/M.Walker; 14 Biofotos; 15 bottom right N.H.P.A; 16 top P.Morris; 17 top P.Morris, bottom right Biofotos; 18 center ZEFA, bottom left N.H.P.A, bottom right, Biofotos; 19 top N.H.P.A, center Nature Photographers, bottom left A.N.I.B, bottom right G.R.Roberts; 20 top Gene Cox, 21 bottom Biofotos; 22 left P.Morris; 23 top right N.Callow/Nature Photographers; 24 left Heather Angel, bottom right M.Chinery: 25 bottom left Heather Angel, bottom right M.Chinery; 26 bottom left British Museum (Natural History), bottom right Gene Cox; 27 left Mary Evans Picture Library, right ZEFA; 28 top and center Crown Copyright (1985), bottom Gene Cox; 29 top ZEFA, bottom left Glaxo Research, bottom right W.H.O; 30 left Dinosaur National Monument, Utah; 31 top left P.Morris, top right Heather Angel, center and bottom right Michael Rubens; 32 top N.H.P.A, center Heather Angel; 33 bottom Gene Cox; 34 top right Gene Cox; 38 bottom left Gene Cox; 39 bottom right J.A.Carter; 41 bottom left Gene Cox; 43 center left Biofotos; 44 bottom left Gene Cox; 46 center Gene Cox; 51 bottom left Biofotos; 52 top P.Morris, center N.H.P.A; 55 top Heather Angel, center Biofotos, bottom right P.Morris; 56 center Gene Cox; 57 top left Heather Angel 58 top British Museum (Natural History); 60 top ZEFA, bottom Anthea Seveking; 61 Robert Harding; 63 Gene Cox; 64 Gene Cox; 67 top Gene Cox, bottom left Burbridge/Nature Photographers, bottom right Brian Hawkes; 68 bottom left Reproduced by kind permission of the Director, Royal Botanic Gardens, Kew, bottom right British Museum (Natural History); 69 center ZEFA, bottom British Museum (Natural History); 71 top Heather Angel; 72 top N.H.P.A, bottom Biofotos; 73 top left N.H.P.A; 74 top A to Z Collection, center G.R.Roberts; 75 Gene Cox; 76 top and center M.Chinery, bottom right Heather Angel; 77 bottom left N.H.P.A; 78 top Robert Harding, bottom left G.R.Roberts; 79 top A to Z Collection; 80 top Heather Angel; 81 top M.Chinery; 82 top Gene Cox; 83 bottom left Heather Angel; 84 center SATOUR, bottom Heather Angel; 85 top Biofotos, bottom right P.Morris; 86 top left Biofotos, top right N.H.P.A, bottom right M.Chinery; 87 bottom M.Chinery; 88 top Biofotos, center N.H.P.A, bottom Heather Angel; 89 center Biofotos, bottom M.Chinery; 90 top N.H.P.A, bottom Nature Photographers; 91 top Brian Hawkes, bottom Kenya Tourist Office; 94 bottom P.Morris; 95 top and bottom ZEFA; 96 top M.Chinery, bottom left N.H.P.A, bottom right A to Z Collection; 98 top N.H.P.A/K.Switak, center Natural Science Photos/Dick Brown; 99 left ZEFA, right Brinsley Burbridge/Nature Photographers; 100 left and right N.H.P.A, 101 bottom right N.H.P.A; 102 top N.H.P.A; 104 top left ZEFA, top right R.G.Argent/N.H.P.A, bottom right Shell; 105 top Greenpeace, center Edward Ashpole, bottom M.Chinery; 106 left Mansell Collection, top right Biofotos, bottom right Imitor; 107 left and center Imitor, right Royal College of Surgeons/G.Rainbird; 108 left M.Chinery, center, top left and bottom left Marc Henrie/Pedigree Chum; 109 top Imitor; 110 top left Biofotos, top right Imitor, center right Institute of Geological Sciences; 111 Zofia Kielan-Jaworowska; 115 center Paediatric Research Unit, Guys Hospital; 120 top Ames Research Laboratory; 121 Imitor; 122 NASA; 123 NASA; 124 bottom Beechams; 125 bottom R.Newsam/University of Kent; 126 University of Birmingham; 127 top Heather Angel, center ZEFA, bottom R.Newsam/ University of Kent;

Picture Research: Jackie Cookson

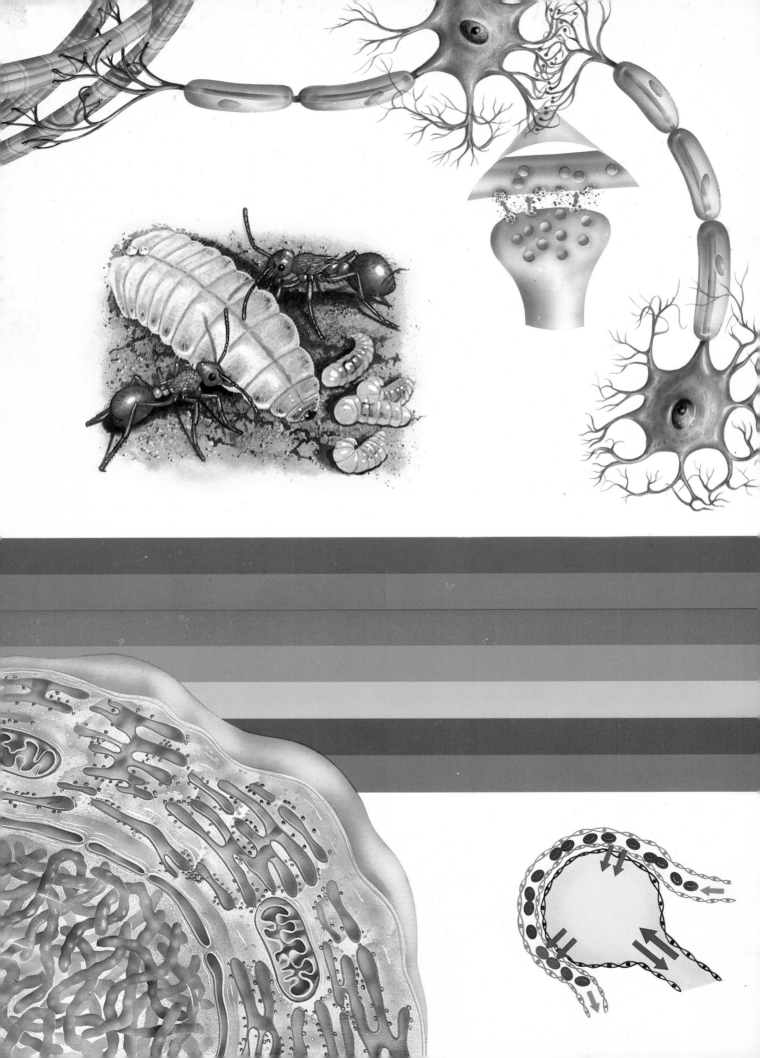